M000096068

RTI *Meets* WRITER'S Workshop

RTI *Meets* WRITER'S Workshop

Tiered Strategies for All Levels of Writers and Every Phase of Writing

LISA MORRIS

CORWIN
A SAGE Company

CORWIN
A SAGE Company

FOR INFORMATION:

Corwin

A SAGE Company

2455 Teller Road

Thousand Oaks, California 91320

(800) 233-9936

www.corwin.com

SAGE Publications Ltd.

1 Oliver's Yard

55 City Road

London EC1Y 1SP

United Kingdom

SAGE Publications India Pvt. Ltd.

B 1/I 1 Mohan Cooperative Industrial Area

Mathura Road, New Delhi 110 044

India

SAGE Publications Asia-Pacific Pte. Ltd.

3 Church Street

#10-04 Samsung Hub

Singapore 049483

Copyright © 2013 by Corwin

All rights reserved. When forms and sample documents are included, their use is authorized only by educators, local school sites, and/or noncommercial or nonprofit entities that have purchased the book. Except for that usage, no part of this book may be reproduced or utilized in any form or by any means, electronic or mechanical, including photocopying, recording, or by any information storage and retrieval system, without permission in writing from the publisher.

All trade names and trademarks recited, referenced, or reflected herein are the property of their respective owners who retain all rights thereto.

Printed in the United States of America

A catalog record of this book is available from the Library of Congress.

ISBN 9781452229928

Publisher: Lisa Luedeke

Acquisitions Editor: Carol Chambers Collins

Associate Editor: Kimberly Greenberg

Editorial Assistant: Francesca Dutra Africano

Production Editor: Eric Garner

Copy Editor: Michelle Ponce

Typesetter: C&M Digitals (P) Ltd.

Proofreader: Laura Webb

Indexer: Sheila Bodell

Cover Designer: Bryan Fishman

Permissions Editor: Jennifer Barron

This book is printed on acid-free paper.

SUSTAINABLE FORESTRY INITIATIVE
Certified Chain of Custody
Promoting Sustainable Forestry
www.sfiprogram.org
SFI-01268
SFI label applies to text stock

13 14 15 16 17 10 9 8 7 6 5 4 3 2 1

Contents

Publisher's Acknowledgments

Corwin gratefully acknowledges the contributions of the following reviewers:

Marsha Basanda
Fifth-Grade Teacher
Monarch Elementary
Simpsonville, SC

Erin Beers
Sixth-Grade Language Arts Teacher
Norwood City Schools
Norwood, OH

Charla Bunker
Middle School Academy Intervention Specialist/Teacher
Great Falls Public Schools
Great Falls, MT

Tracy Coskie
Associate Professor
Western Washington University
516 High Street
Bellingham, WA

Nancy Foote
National Board Certified Teacher
San Tan Elementary School
Higley Unified School District
Gilbert, AZ

Kandace Klenz
Elementary Teacher
NBCT Reading and Literacy
Longview Elementary
Moses Lake School District
Moss Lake, WA

Paulette Moses
Fifth-Grade Teacher
Ballentine Elementary
Lexington/Richland District 5
Irmo, SC

Chuck Perkins
Teacher
Explorer Academy, South Kitsap School District
Port Orchard, WA

Linda Sarver
Retired Elementary Teacher
Excelsior Springs School District
Excelsior Springs, MO

Cathern Wildey, EdD
Professor of BrainSMART Education
Nove Southeastern University
Miami, FL

Gary Willhite
Professor of Teacher Education
University of Wisconsin–La Crosse
La Crosse, WI

Thea Williams-Black, PhD
Associate Professor, Curriculum and Instruction
University of Mississippi
University, MS

Jennifer Wilson
Third-Grade Classroom Teacher
Denver Public Schools
Littleton, CO

1

A Powerful Writing Classroom

*Three Tiers, Three Facets
of Teaching Writing*

"If you have an apple and I have an apple and we exchange apples, then you and I still have one apple. But, if you have an idea and I have an idea and we exchange ideas, then each of us has two ideas."

—Anonymous

When you hear the term Response to Intervention, or RTI, it's a bit clinical, isn't it? When I first heard of it, I assumed it applied strictly to special education and that it is a sweeping, multifaceted initiative that addresses reading instruction, writing instruction, math instruction, you name it. And it is.

But what I hope to show you in this book is that RTI is also in the small moments of our teaching. At the end of the chapter I show you a snapshot view of how blending a writing workshop, best practices, and RTI will create a classroom in which the most struggling writer can persevere. RTI is a multitiered approach to early literacy intervention, and it is also a mindset. It's a way of being in the classroom with children that communicates to each and every child that they are in a learning environment where everyone's talents and needs will be noticed and nurtured. The best teachers respond and intervene continually, each and every school day.

Just as a one-size-fits-all approach to teaching doesn't work, a one professional book covering all topics approach isn't effective either. So in this book I am going to put aside the superwoman tendencies and refrain from covering everything about RTI and focus on RTI in a single curriculum area: writing. And I will zoom in farther and look at RTI within a writing workshop environment.

This is the book I searched for more than four years ago, when I was trying to find guidance on implementing RTI in the writer's workshop. I attended workshops, read up a storm on teaching writing, RTI, differentiation, you name it. What I learned filtered into my teaching. I kept what worked, jettisoned what didn't, and was amazed by how much better my students became as writers and especially those students for whom writing was hard.

I will share with you the step-by-step path of implementing RTI in a writer's workshop.

In each chapter, you'll find practices that work. Here is a break-down of the information available in each chapter.

- In Chapter 1, I provide an overview of RTI and how it looks in its broadest outlines within a writer's workshop.
- In Chapter 2, I address three assessments that will guide your instruction: pre-assessment, formative, and summative assessment.
- In Chapter 3, I provide strategies for making students independent, including checklists and action plans.
- In Chapter 4, I introduce strategies for monitoring students' progress. This is a critical component to RTI.
- In Chapter 5, I focus primarily on the struggling writer and how to differentiate instruction to meet diverse needs.
- In Chapter 6, I examine strategies and techniques that I have found beneficial to all students engaged in the process of writing. The information in this chapter can be used in whole group, small group, or individual instruction.

To some degree, this book assumes a familiarity with the writer's workshop and all the practices that fall under its wing, including minilessons, the writing process, conferring, using writer's notebooks, and so on. It also assumes familiarity with the traits of writing. I provide overviews in Chapters 2 and 6, but I encourage you to check out the following favorite resources in the box below.

TERRIFIC RESOURCES ON TEACHING WRITING

Professional Books

- Culham, R. (2001). *6+1 Traits of writing.* Portland, OR: Scholastic.
- Freeman, M. (1995). *Building a community of writers.* Gainesville, FL: Maupin House.
- Graham, S., MacArthur, C., & Fitzgerald, J. (2013). *Best practices in writing instruction.* New York, NY: Guilford Press.
- Hale, E. (2008). *Crafting writers.* Portland, ME: Stenhouse.
- Morris, L. (2012). *Awakening brilliance in the writer's workshop.* Larchmont, NY: Eye on Education.
- Oczkus, L. (2007). *Guided writing.* Portsmouth, NH: Heinemann.
- Overmmeyer, M. (2009). *What student writing teaches us.* Portland, ME: Stenhouse.
- Routman, R. (2005). *Writing essentials.* Portsmouth, NH: Heinemann.

The "1–2-3" of Best Practices

When I was a kid, 1-2-3 Jell-O was all the rage. It was beyond cool how one could pour and blend a few ingredients in a bowl, chill, and within a few hours have a dazzling three-layered dessert of bright strawberry Jell-O and pink pudding. It makes an apt metaphor here as I think about how teachers expertly fold in best practices and new research into their teaching to create layered, nuanced instruction.

The 1-2-3 layers in this book are RTI, writing process, and the traits of writing—with writing workshop holding the layers in place. I will show you how you can pour all three best practices into your writing curriculum and be richer for it. Before I provide more detail about these three, I think it's good to take a moment to define best practices. For me, best practices are those that research has shown to be effective in a wide swath of educational settings, with a wide array of students. For example, the 6 traits of writing has a solid research underpinning as an assessment that informs writing; the explicit demonstration of writing for real purposes and audiences that is at the heart of writing workshop is also proven by ample research. But beyond the research—and more informally—best practices are the teaching and learning strategies that move the needle on my students' writing achievement. For example, if I can look at a piece of student's writing in February, compare it to a sample from September and can see noteworthy improvement, then best practices have been at work. I like to say they are

---

Think About It

In my own professional development, I would sometimes rush into learning something new without taking the time to think about the beliefs and practices that I had going in to the learning curve. I found that if I take 15 minutes to think about, and maybe jot down, my thoughts on teaching or a particular curriculum area, or how children best learn, it helps me bring new ideas into a defined system of thinking as a practitioner. Ideally, I also have conversations about practice with colleagues. As you think about your current writing curriculum, consider these questions:

- What is good teaching?
- What does good teaching of writing *look* like?
- What does an engaged, effective student writer look like in terms of behavior, participation in the writing time, written work, reading habits?

For me, the concepts that surfaced when I thought about excellent writing instruction were:

- **Rigor:** Is what I am planning to teach sufficiently challenging for all my students?
- **Relevance:** Will my students find what I model or invite them to try something that relates to their lives in a deep way? (Gone are the days of busywork photocopied and pulled from a file); and
- **Relationships:** How does my writing instruction enhance each student's sense of being a part of a writing community in the classroom?

Once I defined these for myself, they became a helpful rubric in my head I used as I planned and taught.

90 percent research based and 10 percent teacher made. That is, as any experienced teacher knows, each teacher is engaged in a continuous action research study: the rich laboratory of his or her own classroom each year.

In this book, I want to encourage you to use your expertise to go on the same journey I did several years ago, when I learned how to fold in widely recognized writing pedagogy with my own teaching.

WHAT IS RTI?

RTI is a multifaceted early intervention approach. In its beginning, it focused on K-2, and particularly on reading, but it also was designed to be used for math and writing, the last of which is the focus of this book. RTI is intended to bring about schoolwide differentiation of instruction with the goal of catching struggling learners before they falter and get left behind.

In writing, RTI incorporates data-based decision making and ongoing progress monitoring into the equation of writing success. It is also about alleviating labels for those students that do struggle. An additional goal of RTI is to reduce the number of unnecessary referrals to Special Education.

According to James B. Hale, PhD (as cited in Gudwin, 2010), the basic ideas of RTI were developed over a century ago. The ideas are relatively simple:

1. The teacher collects data over time and adjusts instruction until the student achieves success.

2. The teacher modifies and differentiates the instruction (intervention) to help a struggling student and then checks regularly (progress monitoring) to see if the intervention is working. If it isn't, the teacher needs to change the intervention and continue progress monitoring. This process continues until the student improves.

3. RTI is what good teachers have always done to help struggling students.

For years, teachers have worked solo in their classrooms with little sharing of data and difficulties. In my opinion, RTI helps teachers unify and work together to meet the needs of all students, not just the ones we personally teach. I look at RTI as not just another program or an added amount of responsibility but as a means to an end . . . ending the labeling and promoting success.

The Tiers

RTI is based on a three-tiered approach to early intervention. These tiers are designed to match each student's needs with layered instruction, immediate feedback, progress monitoring, and ongoing assessment.

A Model of the Tiers

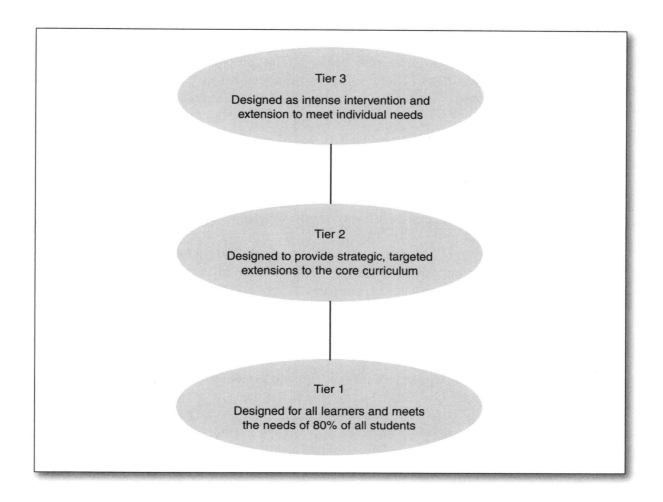

Assessment Frequency

- Tier 3: Twice a month to once a week
- Tier 2: Monthly to twice a month
- Tier 1: 2–3 times a year (quarterly)

Tier 1: General Education

Who: 80 to 85 percent of students

Time: Majority of each day

Format: Whole-group instruction

Let's take a closer look at the three tiers and how they work with our writing instruction.

This is the least intensive of the three tiers. Interventions at this level are provided in addition to general instruction. All students begin in Tier 1 with differentiation included in the instruction. This tier is also referred to as the universal level. In the writing workshop, this would be when the daily minilesson is taught. This lesson is taught to the whole group and is designed to meet the needs of all students. The planning and delivering of minilessons is based on careful formative assessment during small group work, reading through students' writing, and conferring. All students are present for the lesson, hear feedback from other students, and have the opportunity to ask questions and try out the new strategy that was taught. I look at this tier as my *whole group instruction*. As with any instruction, one-on-one assistance is provided to students who need it. This assistance is usually 5 minutes, provided on a needs basis. The assistance provided in this tier can be as simple as answering questions or having an individual writing conference.

Examples of Differentiation within Tier 1:

- I answer individual questions or concerns about the lesson.
- I provide feedback in a conference.
- I redirect any students who seem to be having trouble applying the lesson to their writing.
- I allow another student to work with a student who seems to be struggling.
- I conduct writing notebook checks with feedback for accountability.
- I use the fist of five method after a lesson. Students are asked to respond to questions by showing the number of fingers that represent their level of understanding. A quick glance at the one and two fingers lets me know who I need to assist during conferencing. *One finger shows the lowest level of understanding while five fingers show the highest.*
- I use the thumbs up/thumbs down/thumbs sideways technique that is similar to the "fist of five." If a student understands the minilesson of the day and is having success trying it out in their notebooks or drafts, then a "thumbs up" is given. If a student needs assistance, he or she signals with a "thumbs down." Finally, to signal the student is unsure, a sideways thumb is given. I simply jot down the names of students who show me the thumbs down or sideways signs, and as I walk around during independent writing time, I pay close attention to those names on my list. Sometimes students think they do not understand the concept, but I find that actually they do. And of course the opposite can be true as well.

Tier 2: Targeted Group

Who: 10 to 15 percent of students

Time: 3 to 5 times per week for 15 to 20 minutes

Format: Small group instruction

This is supplemental intervention provided to a small group of students, above and beyond the basic instruction, who have the same or similar difficulties with a particular writing skill or stage of the process. These students are basically performing below the expected levels of accomplishment (called benchmarks). The students in Tier 2 are at some risk of academic failure. It is this tier that a large portion of this book focuses on. The duration of the intervention is 15 to 20 minutes 3 to 5 times per week, depending on the need. Remember that this instruction is in addition to the core instruction. I consider Tier 2 my flexible grouping format. This group frequently changes in a writing workshop. It changes as the curricular needs of the students change. Typically, the interventions are implemented for 2 to 3 weeks and progress monitoring is conducted on a monthly or bimonthly schedule. Students who do not respond need an alternate strategy and additional progress monitoring. If, however, the student fails to make gains and the gap between the student and the achievements of the other students widens, the possibility of testing for special services and intensive instruction available in Tier 3 may need to be considered. This final step, into Tier 3, takes time, a good bit of time. The move from Tier 2 to Tier 3 occurs only after several rounds of supplemental intervention have proven unsuccessful.

Examples of Differentiation within Tier 2

- I use strong or weak student models to emphasize a teaching point.
- I use conversation to spark ideas. (See example below)
- I use peer tutors to reinforce skills and strategies.
- I break down their writing into smaller chunks. (See example on next page)
- I provide effective feedback, focusing on the strengths of the writers as well as the weaknesses.
- I use graphic organizers to help organize thoughts.
- I use mentor texts to provide concrete examples for writing craft or skills.
- I use mnemonic devices such as W5 + H1 (who, what, where, when, why + how) to self-check pieces of writing.
- I schedule group sharing or publishing. *Group sharing and publishing is important because it gives writers the chance to learn from one another. The more feedback a struggling writer receives, the more confidence is built.*
- I provide additional time for any assessments or daily writing requirements

Two Strategies in Action In later chapters I share more strategies in action. Here are two that work with any tier of instruction.

Using Conversation to Spark Ideas

Many of my students who struggle with writing need additional time to talk through their writing. Here is an example of a conversation between myself and Ronnie, one of my students in a Tier 2 small group. The other three students in the group have the opportunity to verbally share as well, but it is my conversation with Ronnie that I will highlight.

Me: Ok, Ronnie, I see that you have used our laminated storyboard to plan this personal narrative. I would like you to tell me your story and use some of the details from the organizer to help you. I may stop you periodically to ask questions that will help you add details and specific point to your writing.

Ronnie: Well, my story began when I was about six years old. I wanted a puppy really bad and I kept begging my parents to buy me one. I gave them lots of good reasons why I needed one. They weren't sure that I was responsible enough but I kept on begging. Finally, my begging paid off.

Me: Oh, I love dogs and you know this. So your topic has my attention. Can you elaborate on a few examples that you gave your parents as to why you needed the puppy?

Ronnie: Sure, I told my parents that I would have a best friend and that I would walk the puppy every day. I also promised really good grades in school.

Me: Let's add those details to your storyboard. This is a great beginning to your story and readers like knowing specifics. Keep going with your narrative.

Ronnie: (After he adds the details) Well, we decided to rescue a puppy. We went to the pound because you (pointing to me) always tell us in class that it's special to rescue an unwanted animal. We loaded up the car and took off. I was very nervous on the way to the pound.

Me: I love that you thought of me when deciding where to get the puppy. I also noted that you were nervous. This is a wonderful place to show the reader what you looked like nervous. Can you describe that to me?

Ronnie: Sure. I was biting my fingernails and kept looking out the window of the car to see where we were. Do you think I should add that to my story map?

Me: Absolutely. That is the strategy of "show, don't tell" and it's important to include this in your writing.

Ronnie went on to finish his story and tell the group all about his new Labrador Retriever with white spots on her ears. They named her Nala, and he has loved her for the last 4 years. The whole conversation took roughly 8 minutes and then it was the next student's turn. It sometimes just takes a little extra support to help struggling writers realize that they have a voice and a story to share.

Breaking the Writing Into Manageable Chunks

To many writers, the task of writing a story from beginning to end seems daunting. For my struggling writers, it seems impossible. I assure them that it is not. Let's look at an expository essay that has five paragraphs. The introduction and conclusion should state the thesis statement (or rewording the prompt in younger grades) and the three reasons of support for the thesis statement. The three middle paragraphs are the meat of the essay. This is where all of the *why* and *how* takes place. I have found that if I take the essay one paragraph at a time, my struggling writers appreciate the manageable chunks and their essays become focused and detailed. Our first step is to plan. All writers must plan. Then I have my Tier 2 students draft their introduction, or the first paragraph. After that initial draft, we revise and edit that introduction. The same process happens with the first point paragraph (or second paragraph of the essay). We continue this method one paragraph at a time. It usually takes 2 to 3 days. The rest of the students work through the process at their own pace. My Tier 2 group is never too far away from the others because I monitor the status of the class and keep everyone focused on the deadline that we have set for the published piece.

> **Tier 3: Intensive Instruction**
>
> **Who:** 1 to 5 percent of students
>
> **Time:** 4 to 5 days a week for a minimum of 30 minutes
>
> **Format:** Small group instruction or pull out

This is the most intensive of the interventions. Individualized instruction takes place, in my classroom or the special education teacher's classroom 4 to 5 days per week for a minimum of 30 minutes of intensive instruction. Ideally, interventions should take place on a daily basis, but my school does not have the supplemental staff, for the area of writing, to support this. It is estimated that 1 to 5 percent of all students need Tier 3 interventions to show a positive response to instruction (Bender and Shores, 2007). The interventions for this level are supplemental to Tier 1 and 2; students still benefit from the Tier 1 instruction. The interventions should be administered in a one-on-one or small group (2 to 3 students) setting with inclusion of special education services. The students who are placed in Tier 3 are at a high risk for failure. If not responsive, these students may be candidates for special education. In my classroom, the students in Tier 3 are served by the speech teacher. While my focus remains on the heart of the instruction, as well as Tier 1 and 2 assistance, a supplemental teacher focuses on the students in Tier 3. We share a common planning period and meet weekly to re-evaluate and plan for additional instruction. If the interventions are working, the supplemental teacher continues to use them, but if the students do not respond a new plan must be created. I am still the teacher on record and I am accountable for the adequate yearly progress these students make, but with a class of 23 (a total of 86) students it is advantageous to have some assistance with the 2 to 3 students who need the extra small group assistance. Typically, the supplemental teacher comes into the classroom on Tuesday, Wednesday, and Thursday. Progress monitoring is administered and evaluated on a weekly or bimonthly basis to determine the effectiveness of the intervention. Interventions are implemented for a minimum of 6 weeks.

Examples of Differentiation within Tier 3:

- I instruct individuals or use small group guided writing.
- I provide additional time.
- I allow students to dictate their stories.
- I allow the use of a computer or Alphasmart—I have several students every year who have been diagnosed with Dysgraphia. *Dysgraphia is a specific learning disability in the area of writing in which students struggle to get their thoughts written down on paper. These students typically have poor handwriting and spend an inordinate amount of time attempting to write simple things.*
- I modify assignments—this may include reducing the amount of writing required or modifying an assignment into smaller chunks.
- I allow the use of tape recording devices to record stories.
- I allow the use of computer programs to help students generate ideas or assist with structure. (Several websites are provided at the end of this chapter.)
- I use strong or weak student models to emphasize a teaching point.
- I demonstrate how to break down writing into smaller chunks.
- I provide effective feedback, focusing on the strengths of the writers as well as the areas of concern.
- I model how to use graphic organizers to help organize thoughts.
- I develop individual spelling lists with the help of my students. I simplify the language of writing prompts when writing on demand (State testing preparation).
- I highlight or color code key words or phrases in anchor papers or individual writing.
- I use mentor texts to provide additional examples for ways to correct an area of weakness.
- I provide examples of mnemonic devices such as W5 + H1 (who, what, where, when, why + how) to self-check pieces of writing.

- I schedule group sharing or publishing.
- I provide additional time for any assessments or daily writing requirements.

Notice how all of the examples of assistance from Tier 1 and Tier 2 are also incorporated into the Tier 3 list. I know that, especially with my struggling writers, the more choices of assistance I have the better chance I have for serving individual needs. The main difference between the assistance of Tier 2 and Tier 3 is the amount of time within the tiered instruction (frequency). The assistance may be the same, but the duration of the assistance will differ.

Keeping it Simple

I have to keep things simple. It is the only way I can keep my sanity with the increase in academic requirements set for our students and ourselves as educators. While looking at interventions and strategies that can help my students, I consider the following questions:

- 1. What is the problem? (DEFINE/PRE-ASSESS)
- 2. Why is this problem taking place? (ANALYZE DATA)
- 3. What strategy/plan can I use that may help solve this problem? (IMPLEMENT)
- 4. Is the strategy/plan working? (EVALUATE/MONITOR)

I know that as long as I keep my focus on the writer—the living breathing component in the classroom—and allow assessment to guide my instruction, then I am much closer to ensuring the success of my students with the difficult task of writing. But I can't do it alone. I understand that parents provide a critical perspective of their child and traditional methods of communication (parent-teacher conferences, meetings, phone calls) are critical to bridge any gaps that may arise between home and school. I often share the quote found at the beginning of the chapter with the parents I come in contact with. To me, it shows that by working and sharing together, teachers, parents, and students, we can make a difference. In Chapter 5, I have included more ways to get parents involved.

I close this chapter one with a snapshot into a classroom where RTI and best practices for teaching writing come together to create an environment conducive to all students.

Welcome to Mrs. A's room. Look around and you will see that there is an abundance of writing material conducive to learning. The bulletin boards are lovingly filled with children's work and displayed with pride. The classroom library is filled with basket after basket of quality books and student-created texts. The students in Mrs. A's classroom are engaged in their writing and there is a sense of accomplishment in the air. Mrs. A is excited about learning and the students are excited too.

During each minilesson, Mrs. A encourages participation, questions, and suggestions. The lessons are focused and created strictly based on the needs of her students. The writers in this room write every day. They understand, because Mrs. A has shown them through her own writing examples, that writing is hard work, but hard work pays off and high expectations can be and are met. Each minilesson is paired with a mentor text that has quality examples of craft specific to the objective of the lesson. These lessons are differentiated based on the interests of her students and she provides depth, not just coverage, within these lessons. Mrs. A knows which mentor texts work best with each lesson because she has studied these books and cherishes them.

The students in this classroom are given time to write. At least 50 percent of their writer's workshop is reserved for writing. Mrs. A also believes in allowing her students' choices about their writing and prompts are rarely used. When you look around you can see that 95 percent of the students are engaged. There is good teaching going on in whole group, small group, and individual settings. Groups are carefully selected based on formative and summative assessments, as well as anecdotal notes. Students are placed into tiers based on thorough evaluations and analysis of any information gathered from assessment and notes.

Mrs. A knows that she is not alone . . . that her RTI team of experts will assist her in her curricular decisions.

The students are taught using the process-oriented instructional model and within that model are opportunities to share. The students in Mrs. A's room share often and freely. No one is afraid of becoming a target; they are all writing partners in this room—partners that belong to a writing community led by a teacher with a passion for teaching and continued learning.

To top it off, the school where Mrs. A teaches is also mindful of the best practices for teaching writing. There is a sense of schoolwide determination that is led by a principal with high expectations and fellow teachers dedicated to their craft. This is a place where all students should be so fortunate to attend. This is an environment and a teacher that gets results and where students thrive. Much of this success is due to the writing workshop atmosphere and the teacher's dedication and desire to reach all students, but there is an added component that is ensuring the success of even the most deficient writers . . . RTI.

Informational Resources

There is a wealth of information on all facets of RTI, not just in the area of writing. What follows are a handful of resources I like.

Professional Books on RTI:

- Allington, R. (2008). *What really matters in Response to Intervention.* Upper Saddle River, NJ: Pearson.
- Applebaum, M. (2009). *The one-stop guide to implementing RTI.* Thousand Oaks, CA: Corwin Press.
- Drapeau, P. (2004). *Differentiated instruction: Making it work.* New York, NY: Scholastic.
- Fisher, D., & Frey, N. (2010). *Enhancing RTI.* Alexandria, VA: ASCD.
- Howard, M. (2009). *RTI from all sides.* Portsmouth, NH: Hrinemann.
- Strickland, D., Ganske, K., & Monroe, J. (2002). *Supporting struggling readers and writers.* Portland, ME: Stenhouse.

Websites

- *www.studentprogress.org* is sponsored through the National Center on Student Progress Monitoring. The website is a national technical assistance and dissemination center for implementation of evidence-based student progress monitoring. Under the "Tools" section, there is a list of eight available tools for progress monitoring that were reviewed by a technical review committee in regard to cost, implementation, and support from the vendor.

- *www.progressmonitoring.net* is sponsored by the Research Institute on Progress Monitoring (RIPM) at the University of Minnesota in collaboration with Iowa State University. The website provides an overview of progress monitoring and, specifically, curriculum-based measurement. The purpose of the RIPM is to conduct research on curriculum-based measurement (CBM) and other related aspects of progress monitoring.

- *www.education.umn.edu/nceo* is sponsored by the National Center on Educational Outcomes at the University of Minnesota. The website is a national resource center for building and designing educational assessment and accountability systems for monitoring results for all students.

- *www.osepideasthatwork.org* is sponsored by the Office of Special Education Programs. The website provides a toolkit on teaching and assessing students with disabilities including current information that will move teachers, educators, and schools forward in improving results for students with disabilities.

- *www.interventioncentral.com* was developed by school psychologist, Jim Wright, and provides many educational resources for both academic instruction and behavior management. Under the "CBM Warehouse" link there are several resources for implementing a progress monitoring system, specifically CBM, including training materials on implementation, CBM probes, research norms for setting student goals, and graphing formats.

- *www.aimsweb.com* is a comprehensive formative assessment system using CBM in reading, early literacy, early numeracy, math, spelling, and written expression. AIMSWEB provides a total package that uses a RTI format for universal screening and ongoing progress monitoring.

- *www.texasreading.org* provides information on scientifically based reading research, research-related information on Vaughn's 3Tier Model of RTI, and materials for all grade levels in the area of reading and language arts.

- *www.readingrockets.org* is a national multimedia project offering information and resources on how young children learn to read. The site is comprised of Public Broadcasting System (PBS) TV programs (video and DVD).

Computer-Based Resources for All Tiers

- Step Up to Writing (www.sopriswest.com)
- Expressive Writing (www.sra4kids.com)
- Reasoning and Writing (www.sra4kids.com)
- REWARDS Writing: Sentence Refinement (www.sopriswest.com)
- Write . . . from the Beginning (www.thinkingmaps.com)
- Co: Writer (www.donjohnston.com/products/cowriter)
- Handwriting Without Tears (www.hwtears.com)
- Spelling Mastery (www.sra4kids.com)

2 Writing Assessments That Help You Plan the Day, the Month, the Year

❧

"The important question is not how assessment is defined but whether assessment information is used."

—Palomba and Banta

❧

Have you ever found that because the education field is so full of buzz words, that in the high speed of teaching, you don't pause to unpack the meaning of a term? Let's take a moment to consider *Response to Intervention (RTI)*. Here's how I distill it: Students respond to our instructional interventions, and then we monitor the quality of their response. We check to see that our intervention, in fact, helped the student progress. In this light, RTI compels us to *use* the assessment information we collect; it helps teachers shift into a higher gear of responsive teaching. As Catherine Palomba and Trudy Banta imply, we are big on testing, but short on intervening in today's classrooms.

When we apply RTI to writing instruction, students' knowledge of writing deepens and their skills strengthen because we intervene and then gauge their response. But in order to intervene with optimal, timely support, we need to have current data that reveal to us the areas where students need extra help. The beauty of RTI is that it provides a framework for gathering, evaluating, and acting on data. It allows an entire school to commit to making sure that classroom teachers and specialists are vigilant about seeing how students respond to the instruction and stepping in to intensify the intervention when needed. When implemented well, there is thoughtful teaching and no guessing. In this chapter I show you how to collect data using three types of assessment used at different points in the school year. I will show you how to make assessment a tool that you use in your classroom that is as handy as a hammer, a pair of scissors, or a tape measure in getting a job done. Assessment informs our instruction, awakens students' self-awareness as learners, and allows us to monitor their progress. To be sure, assessment has an intense, even nerve wracking macro level—statewide testing that grabs the newspaper headlines—but in the pages of this book, it's the micro level that I give the most air time to, for it's the everyday conferring, responding to students' writing, and formative assessments that matter most to students' development as writers.

Defining the Terms

- **Assessment:** Collecting information on the progress of students' learning, often using a variety of procedures.
- **Evaluation:** Reviewing the assessment data and making judgments on the instructional implications of the information.
- **Reporting:** Conveying the results.

To begin, consider how your classroom assessments and your school's approach to assessment measure up to the seven purposes of assessment as defined by Kellough et al. (as cited in Swearingen, 2002):

Seven Purposes of Assessment

1. To assist student learning

2. To identify strengths and weaknesses

3. To assess the effectiveness of an instructional strategy

4. To assess and improve the effectiveness of curriculum programs

5. To assess and improve teaching effectiveness

6. To provide data that assists in decision making

7. To communicate with and involve parents

Think about each item. Would you say it strongly applies to your teaching? Somewhat? Rarely? It's helpful to take the pulse of your current assessment practices and to ensure that assessment is being used to its fullest potential. For example, it took me a while to use assessments as feedback for the effectiveness of my lesson—to realize that assessment is a two-way street. Students are being measured, but my teaching is too.

THE POWER COUPLE: PRE-ASSESSMENT AND FORMATIVE ASSESSMENT

Without writing assessments, there can be no Tier 1, Tier 2, and Tier 3—no differentiated instruction. We need to know precisely who is struggling and precisely what he or she is struggling with. But the assessments needn't engulf the writing workshop and add pressure. In the course of this chapter, I show you that much of what you are already doing in the classroom answers the call of the three major types of assessments. I show you how you can be more strategic in having one build upon another to give you a much clearer path as a writing teacher, week by week. By using these assessments efficiently, there is less teaching in the dark, which is stressful. In this chapter, I focus on three types:

1. Pre-assessment (finding out)

2. Formative Assessment (checking in, feedback, student involvement)

3. Summative Assessment (making sure)

I am one of those people who needs a detailed map and not just in the classroom. I love to travel but I'm not the type to head to Europe and just wing it without reservations or an itinerary. I like having a clear vision of where I want to go, about how long it will take me to get there, and where I will go next. By being prepared, I enjoy the journey much more. The same is true for planning instruction—teaching and travelling are similar processes.

So my first advice to you is to know where you are and how far you have to go. It's quite basic, but a lot of teachers neglect to take the time to work backward from an end goal—whether the end goal is a statewide test in spring or a published narrative in autumn. You have to start with a clear plan and a clear goal.

Go Slow Out of the Starting Gate

I have been teaching for almost 22 years. The last eight years have been at my current school. Several years ago, the school decided to departmentalize. Due to this decision, I am the sole teacher of writing for fourth grade. I have 86 students that I teach this year, at least one-half are from single-family homes. Despite these statistics, my school is one where a sense of community is felt the moment you walk through the doors. Our student population is diverse and its needs apparent. We have a high percentage of students that qualify for free and reduced lunch. The same frustrating situations are felt in my school as in most schools: little parental support, children are hungry and tired, parents are hard to reach, and students' behavioral problems are worse on some days more than others. But through all of these obstacles, our school is a place where learning is expected and expectations are kept high. I tell you all of this to make it clear that there is time, even with difficult situations, to slow down, and pre-assessments helped me downshift.

After I started incorporating pre-assessments into my long range planning and letting this information design my lessons for me, our state writing scores rose from 69 percent to 82 percent to 88 percent and this past year to an astounding 98 percent! My fourth graders, with all their diversity in abilities, home lives, behaviors, and drive, achieved the coveted spot as the highest scoring students in our county (and surrounding counties). They scored higher than any other students in elementary, middle, or high school. It was a well-achieved honor that took time, preparation, and a little more relaxing and reflecting. But the combination worked. And it started with pre-assessment, which I turn to now.

PRE-ASSESSMENT: DISCOVERY OF WHAT STUDENTS KNOW

Pre-assessment or entry-level assessment, for writing is used to determine what students already know and what they need to know. By administering a pre-assessment in the first couple of weeks of school, I get a picture of my class that keeps me from guessing what the next steps will be—instead, I see which writers need support from me first, which writers are proficient enough that I can turn to them a bit later, and so on. Pre-assessments help me see beyond the first tier of whole-class instruction and begin to think about second and third tier students, and how I might help them.

I have to admit, it took me several years to get to the point where I was able to respond to pre-assessment information and tweak my lessons rather than skip merrily ahead with my plans regardless of the actual students in my class! I loved planning. I planned in advance (sometimes *way* in advance) what lessons would be taught and when. I organized every lesson with a mentor text, student samples, graphic organizer, and so on. My lesson plans were a thing of beauty and rarely deviated from the version that I turned in to my principal each week. Sometimes I would really try to impress her and turn in a month's worth of lessons at a time . . . just to show how prepared I was. But, I wasn't prepared at all. I thought I was enlightened, but I might as well have been teaching writing in the dark. By November, I would end up frustrated and confused, wondering why my students were not making the adequate progress they needed to be making.

So what did I do? I simply stopped and slowed down. I know that this concept of slowing down is unheard of in our classrooms. The state mandates tests that loom over our heads and don't allow us to stop. The preprinted programs and curriculum guides push us forward, never backward, and are designed to cover the standards at a holistic rate. But the success my students achieved when I slowed down and let assessments guide my instruction has made all the difference in the world.

Different Types of Pre-Assessment

The following are the main types of pre-assessment that I use in my classroom:

- prompt pre-assessment,
- strengths/weaknesses T-chart (similar to the one in Chapter 3),
- RTI assessment chart,
- grouping map,
- KWL charts,
- student discussions,
- writing samples,
- teacher observations,
- interest inventories,
- conferences, and
- anecdotal notes.

Prompt Pre-Assessment

The first few weeks of school, my writer's workshop is a place of discovery. I am learning who my students are and they are learning all about me. Trust is built, and we all know that if our students trust us, they will work to the absolute best of their abilities. It is also during this time that I assess what my students know and the areas which need focus. One way I do this is with a prompt pre-assessment.

I typically start the year focusing on the personal narrative unit of study. This is one of the genres that is tested in our state-mandated Florida Comprehension Achievement Test (FCAT). The students in my state are given 45 minutes to draft, write, and revise a piece of writing. Given my unit of study and the test looming later in the year, I make the prompt pre-assessment focused on personal narrative, and I align it with the requirements for our state writing test. I even use the official lined paper and the 45-minute time limit. I explain to my students that I need to know what to teach them so I want them to do their very best.

Using the Data to Plan Tier 1 Instruction

After the test is administered, I evaluate the responses. Then I use a simple strengths and weaknesses T-chart to help me document the data. I continue to monitor the strengths I see and build upon them in minilessons, but it is the collective weaknesses *of the group* that galvanize my immediate Tier 1 instruction. (See Chapter 3 for how I use individual T-charts to help students set writing goals and pick up clues as to who needs Tier 2 and 3 instruction.) With RTI it is easy to feel panicky about the need to "tier," but keep in mind, your curriculum remains based on the needs of most of your students—the 85 percent of Tier 1.

With the strengths/weaknesses chart completed, I use it to help me design my units of study curriculum (see following chart). For example, I may see that students need teaching about dialogue and powerful endings, because these attributes were weak in the personal narratives. But I also look for what I am *not seeing* in their writing. That is, what attributes of effective writing aren't in evidence? For example, the ability to elaborate, narrative structure, or speaker tags.

I use both the patterns of errors and the elements I don't see at all to plan future whole-class minilessons and small group instruction. If there are six or fewer students in need of reteaching of a particular skill or strategy, I pull them into a small group. I also note which students may need more intensive support.

Here are the needs I see I have to address:

1. Beginnings that grab the reader

2. Strong verbs to amplify the climactic moment

3. A satisfying ending that makes sense and resonates

4. The correct usage and punctuation of dialogue

5. Adding assonance and onomatopoeia for impact and cadence

6. Creating a rising and falling action sequence in the middle paragraph

7. Basic spelling of sight words

8. Capitalizing a title and making it catchy

I also notice all the strengths, and flag student's pieces—and parts of student's pieces—that I want to showcase, with their permission, in future minilessons.

Planning Chart for Narrative and Expository Units of Study

Take a look at how I map out plans for units of study, as shown in Figure 2.1. I can't emphasize enough the importance of being flexible—that is, don't feel you have to set the plan in stone. That's why you see I make an estimate of the days I will devote to each step of the writing process. (I actually post a schedule in the class because my students benefit from seeing the routines.)

Notice that in the third column, I have included tiered instruction ideas so you can get a sharper sense of how the pre-assessment data inform the writing genre unit, overlaying the writing process with easy accommodations for Tier 2 and Tier 3 students. In essence, the pre-assessment data help me marry craft lessons with skill lessons designed around what I know my students need. Tier 1 students benefit because the instruction responds to their needs as well. The chart at the end of the figure details the RTI notes only for the personal narrative unit; most of the accommodations can be used for an expository as well. The main difference is in the collecting step of the process. For expository writing, many of my Tier 2 or 3 students have difficulties proving *why* or *how* within the body of the essay. A small-group setting and extra time to "prove their points" and add specific details usually is the extent of assistance needed.

Figure 2.1   Long Range Planning

PERSONAL NARRATIVE	6-8 weeks	RTI CONSIDERATIONS
Establishing procedure and routines	5-7 days	
Pre-assessment for personal narrative (prompt)		Extra time given for those with accommodations
Introducing the notebook lessons	10 days	More small group lessons about adding details
Collecting personal narrative ideas	3-4 days	Small group planning for ideas, more time to discuss
Re-reading our notebooks/ notebook dig	1-2 days	
Selecting an idea	1-2 days	Instead of choosing 3 choices, narrow down the choice to 2
Marinating/planning for the idea	3-4 days	Will need an additional day to plan using laminated graphic organizers
Drafting	2-3 days	May draft in chunks; focus on the beginning one day, the middle the next, and the ending another
Revising	2-3 days	Allow extra time to reread and revise
Editing	1-2 days	Sight word charts may be provided

Publishing	1–2 days	
Whole class celebration (sharing):	1–2 days	
Timed personal narrative (with a prompt):	1 day	Extra time will be given for those with accommodations
EXPOSITORY UNIT OF STUDY		
Pre-assessment for an expository essay	1 day	
Collecting expository topics	3–4 days	
Re-reading our notebooks/ notebook dig	1–2 days	
Selecting a topic	1–2 days	
Marinating on the topic	3–4 days	
Drafting	2–3 days	
Revising	2–3 days	
Editing	1–2 days	
Publishing	1–2 days	
Whole-class celebration	1–2 days	
Timed expository essay (with a prompt):	1 day	

Strengths	Weaknesses

Using the Data to Create an RTI Assessment Chart

After I have administered the initial personal narrative prompt and studied the T-chart findings (and of course these same tools work for any genre you are focusing on) I also document the results in an RTI assessment chart. This chart changes slightly as my assessment opportunities grow. At the beginning, about 2 weeks into the school year, it looks like Figure 2.2.

Figure 2.2 RTI Assessment Chart: Personal Narrative

Name	Standardized writing score (from the previous year's state mandated writing test or countywide writing test)	Personal narrative timed pre-test / prompt (formative) Tier 2 (T2) Tier 3 (T3) (Area of need) 1st score/Tier/Retest Score	Personal narrative timed post-test/ prompt(summative) Tier 2 (T2) Tier 3 (T3) (Area of Need) ** Set up RTI meeting for further assistance
Bill	3.0	3.0/T2/4.0 (organization/conventions)	4.0
Kim	2.0	2.0/T2/3.0 (organization/word choice/ conventions)	3.0/T2 (word choice/conventions)
Carl	1.0	1.0/T2/2.0 (organization/voice/conventions/ word choice)	2.0/T2 (organization/conventions/word choice)**

** This information was taken from my initial pre-assessment

When I complete a unit of study on personal narratives and begin to focus my instruction on expository essays, the chart looks like Figure 2.3; notice that the column for a standardized writing score is not evident. This score does not need to be documented twice; it is one score that comes from the previous year. In my case, it comes from the data provided to me by the third grade teachers.

Figure 2.3 RTI Assessment Chart: Expository

Name of student	Expository essay timed pre-test (formative) Tier 2 (T2) Tier 3 (T3) (Area of Need) 1st score/Tier/Retest Score	Expository essay timed post-test (summative) Tier 2 (T2) Tier 3 (T3) (Area of Need) **Set up RTI meeting for further assistance

A Case Study: Bill

At the beginning of the year, I looked through Bill's writing folder from the previous year, perusing writing samples and the countywide writing test. In my school system, only grades 4, 8, and 10 take a state-mandated writing test (FCAT). The other grades take practice tests much like the real thing. Bill's writing test from third grade showed me that he scored on grade level with a 3.0 score. I wrote this score under the *Standardized Writing Score* in the RTI Assessment Chart (Figure 2.2).

In fourth grade, the students must score a 4.0 on the state test in order to be proficient. I gave my entire class a personal narrative prompt and 45 minutes to respond to that prompt. These are the testing conditions of our FCAT. These are the same testing conditions used for the countywide writing test. I collected the personal narrative pre-assessment tests and filled out a strengths and weaknesses chart (Figure 3.1 in Chapter 3) to help me plan for my unit of study on personal narratives. I looked closely at the weaknesses I observed and documented to guide my instruction. Then it was time for me to target students who were unable to score a 4.0 on this fourth grade pre-assessment. I noted that Bill scored a 3.0 so I knew that he would need a strategic intervention and further progress monitoring to ensure his success as a writer. But I needed to look closely at precisely which *area of writing* he was having the most difficulty with.

I use (and our state does as well) a 6 Traits rubric to holistically and analytically score a student's writing. The 6 Traits can be taught as you demonstrate and move through the writing process. The 6 Traits are:

- ideas,
- organization,
- voice,
- sentence fluency,
- word choice, and
- conventions.

Here's how I merge the writing process and the 6 Traits together. Naturally, there is nothing hard and fast about this match-up; for example, you could find a golden opportunity to teach about voice during the revision stage, or teach about organization during the revision stage. Take your cues from what you see each day in students' performance (see Figure 2.4).

Figure 2.4 Writing-Process Phases and Possible Trait Connections

Phase of the Writing Process	Possible Trait Connection
Prewriting/planning	Ideas Voice (author's purpose) Organization
Drafting	Organization
Revising	Sentence fluency Word choice
Editing	Conventions
Publishing	Presentation (not curricular based)

I saw that Bill scored lowest in the areas of organization and conventions. So I had a plan as to where to start. I decided to tackle the area of organization first and then target the conventions issue during conferences so that his instruction in that area was prescriptive for his personal needs. In Chapter 3, I focus extensively on spelling probes and individualized spelling lists for those students who need it. In my experience, organization and conventions are two very common areas of need among struggling writers (Chapter 4 focuses more on the struggling writer). Because organization and the stage of planning are closely related, I looked at Bill's plan and noted that he had used a web. From experience I know that, for my lowest writers, a web is an unorganized mess of thoughts. They need to see structure and a web doesn't offer this. I like to use the example of a grocery list. If I went to the store with a web of all of the items I needed, I would leave the store without most of them or just decide not to look at my web and randomly start shopping. But if I categorize the items in my web (frozen, fruits, dairy, etc.) then my chances of success are much better. I explain this "storm and sort" strategy in more detail in Chapter 6. I looked again at the rest of the class to see who else might be gathered in a small group to get more intensified instruction.

After evaluating the rest of the class, I find a pattern of needs (Kim and Carl struggled with organization too). I grouped these students together for additional assistance during our 35 minute independent writing time. I show Bill, and the others who were having difficulty with organization, the storm and sort strategy. I allowed them to add details to their existing web and then sort those details in a beginning, middle, and end (BME) chart (shown in Chapter 6). I spent roughly 15 minutes with this group for 2 days. After the small group session each day, I dismissed the students and asked them to go to their special spots for independent writing. I picked up my conferring clipboard and was able to fit in four conferences with the other students who had been working while I was in small group.

After meeting for 2 days, sharing our webs, having small group conferences, and completing the BME charts, I gave the students the opportunity to retake the assessment. I used the same prompt and the same testing procedures as the initial test. I stapled the first and second attempts together and placed the writing in the students' assessment folders. I did not administer this test; rather the supplemental teacher that I have a few days of the week gave the test to the students for me. That way I was able to concentrate on my conferences with other writers.

Bill was able to pull his initial score of a 3.0 up to a 4.0 and when it came time to give another timed test, this one of a summative nature, he was still proficient with a personal narrative. As for his conventions, I continued to administer the spelling probes and continued to see growth in that area.

Creating a Grouping Map for Student Writing

I am not sure how I could teach writing without showcasing the phases of the writing process and the 6 Traits. As shown earlier, the 6 Traits complement the writing process. One method that I use for a quick formative assessment is a grouping map (See example on next page). On the inside of a file folder, I divide the area into six sections, one for each trait. Using the pre-assessment, I evaluate the areas of strength and weakness. Let's look at Bill again. On the RTI Assessment chart for narrative, I recorded that Bill was having difficulty with the traits of organization and conventions. I place sticky notes (the very small ones) with Bill's name on them and put one under the category of *organization* and one under the category of *conventions*.

Example of a Grouping Map

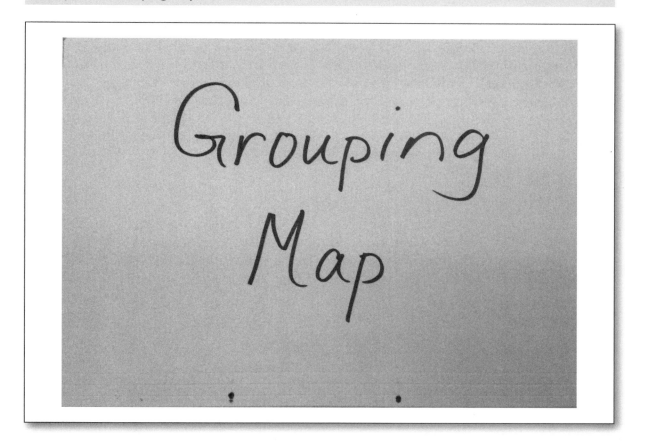

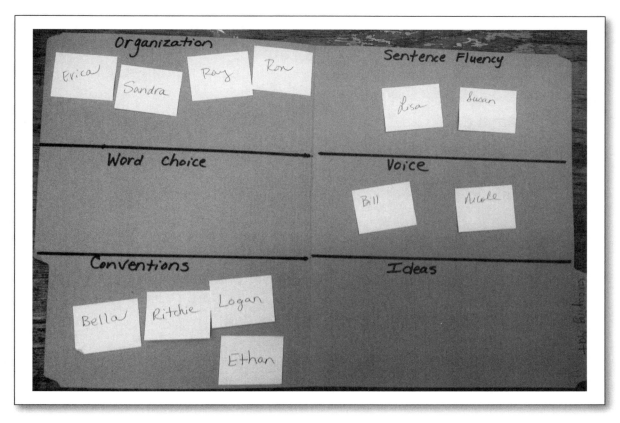

During my small RTI Tier 2 group, or anytime I pull a small informal group, I can see the targeted skill that needs my focus. The visuals with the grouping map are also very telling. After pre-assessing my entire class, or classes, I can quickly open up the grouping map and immediately note the area that I need to holistically target, not just in small groups. For example, if after an assessment and completion of the RTI assessment chart, along with the sticky notes in place on the grouping map, I see that I have 10 names under the category of organization, I know that this is an area for Tier 1, whole-group attention, because a big enough percentage of students are wrestling with it. But, if I see that only five students are in need of additional assistance with the category of word choice, I gather a small group.

ADDITIONAL WAYS TO PRE-ASSESS

The strategies that follow are excellent for not only pre-assessment but for formative assessment as well. The more strategies teachers have in their "toolbox" the better prepared they are to collect data and use it for teaching.

KWL Charts

Before any unit of study, I want my students to build upon their pre-existing knowledge of the study. Let's use the personal narrative example again. Before I begin teaching (and even planning for) this unit of study, I ask for my students to complete a KWL chart in their writer's notebooks. My goal is to find out what they already know (K), what they want to learn (W), and after the unit of study, what they have learned (L). The "what they know and want to learn" drives my instruction. The "what they have learned" is a valuable formative assessment tool. Simple? Yes. Effective? Yes! I get a glimpse into my students' brain for just a moment. A simple chart like this assesses the students without a grade. It lets me know where they are and where they need to go (Figure 2.5).

Figure 2.5 Student Sample: KWL Chart

Know	Want to Know	Learned

Student Discussions

Talking–our classrooms need a lot more of it. And I don't mean the "What did you do last weekend?" chit-chat, even though getting to know our students is a critical component to teaching. I mean authentic conversations about writing. I want to know my students' likes and dislikes. I need to know which students write at home for fun, creating plays with siblings, whodunits, silly family stories, or soulful journal entries. I need to know those students who actually fear writing at school and at home and gently try to find out where the fear comes from. I provide them with the same information based on my own likes and dislikes. Our class discussions not only allow students to self-express on an emotional level but on a curricular one as well. Classroom talk builds trust and with trust comes candor that helps me be a better writing teacher. I never force a student to share, but I take risks myself to draw them out. For example, I might tell them about the time a family member read my journal that I had hidden under my mattress as a girl and how mad I was to elicit a conversation about respecting a writer's privacy; or I may share about feeling crummy because my friend in second grade wrote a poem that was so good, and everyone in class liked it; or about writing a play with friends based on a TV sitcom and performing it in class and how wonderful it was to make people laugh with my writing. The more we share the scary, sad, funny, and thrilling times as writers ourselves, the more our students see the possibilities for their own identities as writers.

On a curricular level, inviting student participation keeps us from talking at students all day. Research shows that teachers do far too much talking, and it impedes learning. The brain that works is the brain that learns.

To jumpstart conversation, I often read aloud something short—a poem, a quote, a picture book, or a passage from the genre or subgenre we are focusing on. For example, before I begin to teach a unit of study on poetry, I want to make sure my students and I "talk poetry" for a while, so I read aloud a few Shel Silverstein poems (or any poet for that matter, he is just one of my students' favorites). I then ask, "What did you notice? Tell me all the things you know about poetry." Some of my students may know quite a lot and others not so much. The purpose is to allow students time to think about what they do know. They are often surprised and delighted about how much they know. And think about the Tier 2 and Tier 3 writers—how beneficial this conversation is for them.

I record the take-aways from these discussions on an anchor chart that evolves as the unit of study gets under way and we learn more. The chart, *"What We Know About Poetry"* is an instant goldmine for me—I can evaluate the collected responses to determine what my students know about the basics of writing poetry, the terminology that goes with the unit, and the patterns and fluency needed to write poems. I think about what I *do not see* on the discussion chart, too, as these attributes of the genre will need to be introduced in whole-class minilessons.

Writing Samples

I am not sure if I could effectively teach writing without using writing samples. These samples are also known as anchor papers. I have a binder of student writing samples for narrative and a separate binder for expository, each organized by genre and score—no student names attached. I have spent a good bit of time evaluating and collecting these samples over several years, and it's been well worth the effort. Within these binders I have put all "like scores" together for easy reference. If I need to show my students an expository essay with a score of 4.0, I can simply go to the expository binder, find the tab labeled 4.0, and select a sample. Where do I find these student samples? I find them in the following places:

1. the Florida Department of Education website (or you state's website),

2. the CD of samples sent to my school of the previous year's FCAT results, and

3. student samples that I have copied (with permission) and scored for an assessment.

When I conduct workshops for my county, I am always asked just how I use these samples to teach writing. The answer is simple; I guide my students to recognize the good and the not so good moments in these papers. We always look for the positive first. These responses from students can be recorded on a piece of chart paper or in a writer's notebook. I like to show my students a simple T-chart with a smiley face on one side and a frown face on the other (see Figure 2.6). The ☺ side is for the good writing and the ☹ side is for areas noted that need to be improved. After we evaluate what the writers did well (the craft), we look for areas that need to be fixed up and determine how to go about doing this (refer to Figure 2.4). I know that when I can get my students to recognize good writing, my chances are better that they will add these craft moments to their own writing. Students who struggle with writing need the visual examples to help them see and apply.

Figure 2.6 Strengths/Areas of Need

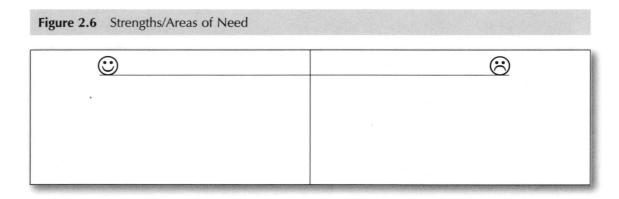

Teacher Observation

I have to know my writers on a personal level (see Figures 2.7 and 2.8). I need to know what topics they enjoy writing about, and they need to know the same about me. I also need to know if they are attempting the new skills presented in the minilesson each day. One way to make sure that application is evident is to observe writers as they write. It sounds simple enough, right? Well, sometimes our enemy, time, can tempt a writing teacher to work on the stack of essays and stories that is piled up on the desk. Believe me, I have had to literally force myself to look away from my desk at all of the work that has miraculously piled up on my desk, calling my name, and venture out into the workshop area where my students are writing.

To me, observing students is almost like football practice before the big game. I need to see, on a daily basis, that the students are getting it and applying it before it's time for a timed writing test or the revision of a published piece. Observation assists teachers in gathering evidence of student learning to inform instructional planning and can serve as feedback to the students as well.

Let me give you an example. If I teach a minilesson on strong verbs, I need to observe my students practicing using strong verbs right away. A simple observation of how well my students understand and apply the lesson objective that day can be viewed during independent writing. I can keep a simple running list of who is applying this skill and who isn't. This list can help me form any small groups. Any students who are in need of extra assistance through RTI need to be spotted right away before I continue with more minilessons. The last thing I want is for a struggling student to feel overwhelmed and give up. Getting them back on track and feeling confident in their writing can be a daunting task . . . so I do all I can to avoid this type of situation. I believe teacher observation can not only benefit the students but also give the teacher a clear road map of what needs to be corrected right away and what needs to be taught later on down the minilesson road.

Figure 2.7 Interest Inventories

Name _____ Date _____

Individual Interest Inventory for Writing

1. One thing I'm good at is _____
   _____.

2. One person who is very special is _____
   _____.

3. A good thing I did was _____
   _____.

4. I laugh when _____
   _____.

5. I want to learn more about _____
   _____.

6. My favorites:

animal _____

sport _____

food _____

TV show _____

game _____

subject _____

special _____

book _____

movie _____

Figure 2.8   Student Writing Attitude Survey

Name _____ Age _____ Date_____ Teacher_____

1. **I like to draw.**
   not at all   a little   some   a lot   a whole lot

2. **I like writing stories.**
   not at all   a little   some   a lot   a whole lot

3. **Writing is boring.**
   not at all   a little   some   a lot   a whole lot

4. **I like to write in my spare time.**
   not at all   a little   some   a lot   a whole lot

5. **I enjoy writing notes, emails, and letters to people.**
   not at all   a little   some   a lot   a whole lot

6. **I like writing at school.**
   not at all   a little   some   a lot   a whole lot

7. **I have trouble thinking about what to write.**
   not at all   a little   some   a lot   a whole lot

8. **It's fun to write things at home.**
   not at all   a little   some   a lot   a whole lot

9. **I like to share my writing with others.**
   not at all   a little   some   a lot   a whole lot

10. **I wish I had more time to write at school.**
    not at all   a little   some   a lot   a whole lot

11. **I like to read.**
    not at all   a little   some   a lot   a whole lot

12. **I think I'm a good writer.**
    not at all   a little   some   a lot   a whole lot

13. **I like to write.**
    not at all   a little   some   a lot   a whole lot

14. **How often do you write at home?**
    not at all   a little   some   a lot   a whole lot

15. **What kinds of things do you write? (genres, topics, or titles)**

_____
_____
_____
_____
_____
_____

Conferences

I will readily admit that conferring with my students used to be difficult. I think I tried too hard. I worried too much about asking the just right question and expecting the just right response. Then I read Carl Anderson's book, *How's it Going?* and a realm of relaxation just surrounded me. I, once again, realized the beauty of keeping things simple. So I began with that general question that Mr. Anderson suggests: "How's it going?" and it worked!!! I relaxed and so did the students. The expectations were still there but the feedback was authentic and genuine. There are several types of conferences. Each holds a place in the writing workshop. As for RTI, this is a valuable formative assessment. It lets the teacher know who knows what, who needs help, and who is mastering the new skill that was introduced as well as who has mastered the cumulative skills that are needed to layer writing. Here are brief descriptions of the types of conferences that I use to let me know how to help my students.

Types of Writing Conferences

There are several different types of conferences that a teacher or student can use and each type of conference serves a particular purpose.

Whole-class sharing: This is an informal type of conference where all of the students listen and give positive feedback to the writer. We gather at our meeting area for these conferences and the writer sits in the author's chair. I like to record the compliments or suggestions that the other students make on a large sticky note. Then, when the writer is finished, I give the comments to him or her and to use later during independent writing.

Quickshares: A quickshare is simply that. Students are asked to pick one line or one small section from a piece of writing and we simply go around the room sharing out loud. I will often ask one or two students to briefly comment after each writer shares. This type of conference usually occurs at the end of writer's workshop. My students love this type of conference because they thrive on sharing and get excited when asked to locate "that one small exceptional moment" in their writing.

Self-conferring: I like my students to be independent thinkers and writers. I provide them with a self-assessment checklist that helps them ask questions of themselves. This is a good way for students to consider what is going well and what concerns exist. A couple of examples of questions that I have on the checklist are:

- Is my topic clear?
- Did I use details?
- Are the punctuation and capitals used correctly?
- What creativity skills did I use? (alliteration, simile, personification, etc.)
- Is my conclusion interesting?

One-on-one formal conferences: The one-on-one conference occurs when I am sitting with one student focused on one piece of writing. What I am addressing with this student depends on where he or she is at in the writing process. Most of my anecdotal notes come from the one-on-one conference. This is the conference where I focus on a strength, ask guiding questions, and then teach a skill, strategy, or technique. If I begin to see patterns of problems, I can address those in a small group conference. This one-to-one style of conferring is the type of conference that most teachers seem to be familiar with.

Roving conference: This type of conference is what I refer to as a "conference on the run." I also refer to this as my ten minutes of research. It gives me the chance to assess the room quickly and determine the status of the class before deciding which student or possibly group of students that I will confer with first. I take notes if I see a student who is distracted or hasn't progressed through to the next step in the process for several days. This may be the student I want to focus on first when it's time for the one-on-one conferences, which usually follow the roving conference. Please note that the entire roving conference takes about ten minutes. Not ten minutes per child but ten minutes for the class as a whole. You will be amazed at how much you notice and document by simply walking around the room.

Small group conferences: There are times that I am able to group students together and teach one particular skill that needs to be addressed. I form these small group conferences based on my findings from either the one-on-one conferences or my roving conference. It is during group conferences that I am able to use much of my conferencing time. I like to have no more than five students in a group conference.

Process conference: This conference is based on what step a student may be in with regard to the writing process. I like to look at each step in the process as a separate curricular planning opportunity. I know that each step of the process merges together to reach the goal of publication, but there are so many subskills within each step that it helps me to look at them categorically when I conference. We want to teach students to be aware of their own writing process. In this conference the teacher allows students to voice their strategies.

Evaluation conference: After I have scored published papers, I sit down with each individual student and go over the strengths, the weaknesses, and some suggested strategies for improving those weaknesses. I use my anecdotal form (Figure 2.9) when I assess and even let the student see my notes. I want my students to understand why they scored what they scored, strategies I would like to see them repeat on the next paper, and of course some areas to improve.

Anecdotal Notes

Anecdotal notes are an excellent way to keep track of our students' thinking. I can't literally get inside those brains, but I must know what they are thinking, how they are working, and how they are processing the new (and old) information. A great deal of attention is being paid to assessment, especially with the inclusion of RTI, and how assessment guides instruction and monitoring. I love to watch my students. I enjoy watching their brains process. I know many teachers go into the field of education for the love of children; I went into the field for the curiosity of how the brain digests information and how in a class of 25 students, they all learn and react to the stimuli of information in 25 different ways. It is truly amazing. By observing the writing process of my students I can record their different learning modalities. I can interpret my recordings and make curricular decisions based on what I see my students doing. Anecdotal notes are very telling. They give the teacher the chance to observe and learn, on a daily basis, how each student individually learns . . . differentiation at its best. After teachers have developed a firm knowledge base of their students they can rely on observations to help place students in RTI groups or provide any one-on-one assistance that may be needed. I use a simple chart for my anecdotal notes and I record what I see. It's a little different than a conference because I am literally watching and reflecting. I make each student an anecdotal notes page so that I can place individual notes in a student's assessment folder. Let me give you a couple of entries from an anecdotal notes page I recently used (Figure 2.9).

Figure 2.9 Anecdotal Notes: Gabby

Initial Observation/Date	Follow-Up Observation/Date	Strategies Taught
09/21/2011 Wrote a mystery and used "tick tock tick tock" for the sound of the clock. She has an excellent grasp of language and is vivid in her descriptions: dreary, scary, intense, thumping of the heart.	09/28/2011 Gabby continues to use awesome adjectives in her writing. I would like to see her branch out and use more creativity skills.	09/28/2011 I showed Gabby the book, *Owl Moon,* by Jane Yolen. She looked through it and took notes in her writer's notebook addressing the multitude of literary devices she found (e.g. similes, onomatopoeia, personification).

Keaton: Had to gently remind him not to grip his pencil so tightly . . . relax . . . writing uses muscles and they take time to develop. He may want to try a pencil grip to help him.

Trevor: Noted that he is constantly erasing . . . so I gave him a drafting pencil (a pencil with no eraser) and told him to just let those thoughts flow. Focus more on the writing not the product.

Tristan: Reminded him to keep that pencil point on the paper. I used the crab and net analogy. He understood and as I observed a little later, he had that pencil lead prepared to write down ideas.

Let me take a moment to explain the crab and net analogy. If you are hunting for crabs and you have the net lifted in the air, in your mouth, or anywhere other than the edge of the water, the chances of catching a crab are slim. You need the net ready . . . right there available for the capture. The same is true for writing. Ideas come and go quickly (like the crab) and if you don't have your pencil ready (on the paper) to catch a thought, you just might have to watch it swim away. This simple analogy helps the students see that even the simplest act of engagement can help them with their writing. It's the attitude of trying and pushing one's self that creates successful lifelong writers.

Anecdotal notes are open-ended and allow the teacher to determine and record what details are important and use the information and data to set instructional goals for the students.

FORMATIVE ASSESSMENT: ASSESSMENT IN THE MIDST OF LEARNING

Formative assessment is the missing link in writer's workshop. Note that the pre-assessment strategies earlier also function as formative assessment. The beauty of these strategies is that they can be used again and again in diverse ways. It isn't always *what* strategy you use but *how* you use it. Too many times teachers and students do not get the opportunity to see how they are doing throughout the writing process. Most evaluations and grades are typically based on a published piece. With formative assessment the needs of the students *throughout the writing process* are monitored, lessons are either developed, or adjusted, and next steps planned.

Formative assessment guides and adjusts my teaching and provides an opportunity for students to identify their own weaknesses or gaps in their learning. Formative assessment basically answers three questions:

1. What do we want students to know?

2. How will we know if they know it?

3. What will we do if they don't?

Formative assessment is particularly valuable for measuring how students are progressing towards learning goals because the results of this type of assessment provide the student with immediate feedback and helps the student (and the teacher) know what to do next.

One point to make clear is that grades are rarely used during formative assessment. I like to use a check plus, check, and check minus method to hold my students accountable.

Exit Card

Frequency: 2 to 3 days a week

The exit card is a quick yet efficient way to gather information about academic readiness. This simple assessment is an excellent way to see if the minilesson stuck and help guide future planning. At the end of a lesson, a teacher can ask either a generalized question or a very specific one based on the day's minilesson. For example, if I taught the skill of adding strong verbs to writing for that day's minilesson, before my students leave, I can simply ask them to write me four sentences using four different strong verbs. I collect the responses as my students leave, read them, and see how many understood the lesson and how many may need additional help the following day. This is an example of a specific type question. A more general question could be "What did you learn today that made you a better writer?" I use both types of questioning several times during the week. It helps me evaluate my plans and what I need to prepare for the next day's instruction.

"I Learned" Statements

Frequency: 1 to 2 days a week

This formative assessment is one of my favorites. It is quick, easy, and informative. I simply use scraps of paper that I have collected. I know several teachers who use index cards, but I have 85 to 100 students and that can get costly. I ask my students to write the words, "I learned" at the top of their strip of paper and then give them 5 minutes to recall and write down everything that they learned from the day's lesson. We take a couple of minutes to either share as a whole group or with an elbow partner. I collect these "I learned" statements and read them after school. I can see what information seemed to be retained the most and if some of the information needs to be addressed again at the beginning of the next day's lesson. This technique is a wonderful way to activate prior knowledge and then build upon this knowledge.

"Thumb It" Strategy

Frequency: Daily or 3 to 4 days a week

My students love this quick assessment. It is a simple thumb up, thumb down, or thumb to the side type of visual cue. If a student gives me a thumbs up I know he is comfortable with moving from the instruction and applying to his independent writing. A thumb down is a quick sign of confusion and anyone with this sign will need to be immediately and directly pulled into a group for clarification. For the students who give a thumbs to the side gesture, I feel comfortable asking them to verbalize their questions and, as a group, we offer assistance and guidance, which usually fixes the potential problem.

Windshield Checks

Frequency: 1 to 2 days a week

I copy the sample cards on cardstock and laminate for durability. After teaching a minlesson, I simply ask my students if they understand the lesson and feel prepared to practice the skill the lesson focused on during independent writing. The students hold up one of the cards and let me quickly assess who understands, who may have questions, and who may need more intensive instruction in a small group setting (Figures 2.10–2.12).

Figure 2.10

CLEAR

"I get it!!!"

Figure 2.11

BUGS

"Some parts are unclear!

Figure 2.12

MUD

"I still don't get it!!!

Yes/No Cards

Frequency: 1 to 2 days a week

Creating Yes/No cards is simple. I glue a large red index card to the back of a green one. On the red side I write the word "NO" in large letters and on the green side I write "YES!" As I teach my minilesson, I periodically stop and check the status of the class. A simple show of a sea of red cards lets me know I need to stop before going any further. If there are just 3 to 4 students who show the "NO" sign I can pull them after the lesson and work further in-depth to answer any questions or show more examples of the concept I am teaching.

Another twist on this formative assessment is to ask questions pertaining to the lesson and a quick check around the room lets me know if my students are on track with the skill. For example, if my minilesson for the day was adding similes to writing to show comparisons, I can ask, "Is the example sentence a simile? The earrings were sparkly like diamonds."

I hope to see a majority of the class holding up the green "YES" side of their cards. If I see a couple of students who do not recognize the example as a simile, I can help them on the spot or let the conversation amongst the class as to *why* this is indeed a simile continue. But, if further clarification is needed, I can meet with a particular student or group of students during independent writing time.

Meet the Press

Frequency: 1 to 2 days a week

Formative assessment is designed to provide feedback to students and shows the teacher, as well as the students, how they are progressing with the skills being taught. One of my favorite approaches is a questioning strategy we call Meet the Press, because it's a chance for the students to grill me like political reporters grill the president after a speech. I ask my students to draw a question mark at the top of their notebook paper. Then I provide them with approximately 5 minutes to ask me any questions about anything I have taught, not only that day but any previous days as well. This strategy is especially great for checking for understanding within each phase of the writing process. For example, if I teach several lessons about strategies students can use during the editing step of the process, then their questions need to be centered on the editing step. I collect these papers, read them, and answer their questions. If I see that the same question has been asked by several students, I can pull these students to the side the next day or make sure I take the time the next day to review the skill that many students seemed to have questions about.

Graffiti Fact

Frequency: 1 to 2 times a month

The word graffiti comes from the Greek word *graphein* which means to write. My students enjoy this tidbit of information before I model and explain the process to them. I place a large piece of chart paper or white bulletin board paper on a table. I have plenty of writing supplies handy (pens, colored markers, etc.). Students are invited to write or draw what they already know about the topic or target goal (for example, similes or poetry). After the students, in small groups, add thoughts, ideas, and even questions to the graffiti chart, students sign their work. This allows me to see, at a glance, any misconceptions, prior knowledge, and learning targets.

Traffic Light Cards

Frequency: 1 to 2 days a week

I must keep things pretty simple in my classroom, and that includes formative manipulatives that my students use. I jokingly tell teachers at the workshops I conduct that I am *not* the Martha Stewart of the writing workshop. For this formative assessment, I give each student a zip top baggie and three index cards; a red one, a green one, and a yellow one. After a minilesson, I ask my students to rank their understanding of what we have been studying by holding up one of their colored cards.

Green: I understand this very well

Yellow: I need some support but understand the basics

Red: HELP! I don't understand!

Fruitful Feedback

Frequency: Daily

My students crave feedback—constructive feedback. I know from my own school days that red pen feedback undermines the writer. Too many teachers today still have that approach, even if they know not to use a red pen. I've seen personal essays with fabulous lead sentences corrected and drained of voice by well-meaning teachers who are trying to train students to adhere to conventional openings like "The most important reason I like . . . "As we read and respond to student papers, we have to be careful to not go on autopilot and try to make our students' pieces conform to safe norms that may be good for writing tests but aren't authentic writing.

I believe that talking about writing and giving specific, fruitful feedback is invaluable in not only determining what our students need but also in celebrating what they have achieved. By fruitful, I mean that my feedback and peer-to-peer feedback has to bear fruit—it has to make the writer blossom and produce rather than wither on the vine from feeling criticized.

The simple sharing T-chart I showed you earlier can be a valuable tool for assessment. As a teacher, I can easily read the comments that the students documented on the T-chart and get a clear sense of the writerly language that is being used and the specific skills that are being attempted. Not only do I ask my students to be specific during the time of sharing but also when we study mentor texts. If a student can recognize and name a strategy or technique that another writer is using, then there is a greater likelihood that this student will also apply what he has noticed in his own writing. But I must go further than that.

Teachers have to assess. And by using formative assessment, from the examples shown earlier, teachers have a clear handle on how well their students are doing. This assessment is authentic because it comes straight from the students' writing. The feedback that I give my students must be specific and authentic and also come straight from the students' writing. This feedback becomes as individual as our students are. There is no learning from comments like "Good job, Jill." To Jill, good could mean many things. Instead, an effective writing teacher needs to look at Jill's writing and document a specific strength and specific weakness and sit down beside Jill and talk about her writing.

Eight Principles of Effective Feedback

1. Be clear with your feedback and how the "next steps" of learning will be implemented.

2. Think carefully about your verbal and written feedback. The goal of feedback is to focus on strengths while assisting in areas of need.

3. Always provide students with a clear learning objective or intention.

4. Make sure the feedback points out clear and manageable steps. Give only 1 or 2 ways in which the work can be improved.

5. Allow students time to absorb the feedback from you as well as from other students.

6. Make sure students understand that feedback will help them improve not only their current piece of writing but will help towards setting longer term goals or targets.

7. Feedback is documented on sticky notes, anecdotal notes, or thought bubbles. Rarely is a piece of writing written on directly.

8. Students are given the opportunity to assess themselves (thought bubbles) and to assess others (sticky notes) as well as dialogue with the teacher (anecdotal notes).

Time-Saving Tips for Formative Assessment

- Know what you are looking for.
- My minilessons are my targeted skills I am looking for.
- Have students highlight examples of the minilesson in their writing.
- Again, the minilessons keep my students focused on what to try and what I am looking for.
- When conferring with a student, skim the paper.
- I will carefully read the paper during the summative assessment.
- Use sticky notes to write comments to students about a piece of writing.
- As I observe my students, I write comments on sticky notes, then I can use these notes to group my students with like instructional needs.
- Look for patterns in student's work.
- This is how I know what to teach.

"Jill, I was impressed with how vividly you described the setting in your beginning paragraph of this personal narrative. It grabbed my attention because my grandmother lived on a farm too.

The use of "weeping willows" and "pastures as far as the eye could see," painted a picture in my head.

Let's take a closer look at how you are punctuating your dialogue. Remember when the class studied the book Stellaluna? Let me get that book out for you again and I would like you to review the correct way to punctuate dialogue."

At that point, I have given Jill a strength and a targeted area she needs to work on. I also gave her the tools (in this case the picture book) necessary to help her correct the area she needed to in her writing. How does this connect to RTI? It depends. If I met with Jill in a one-on-one conference, then I would consider this a Tier 1 type of intervention. Now if I pulled a group of 3 to 4 other students, all struggling with punctuating dialogue, then a little more instruction may be needed and so I would think more in terms of a Tier 2 strategy. My Tier 3 students, however, may have more extensive issues with simple sentence construction as well as applying and punctuating dialogue, so in that case, I would need several days to back up and review sentence structure, then layer my teaching to show these students how dialogue is punctuated. It all depends on what your students need and meeting those needs either one-on-one, in a small group for one to two brief meetings, or in a small group with more foundational teaching and layering over the course of several days.

SUMMATIVE ASSESSMENT: ASSESSMENT AFTER LEARNING

Summative assessment is the end product and fulfillment of an objective. For writing, it is often a published piece or timed writing assignment to a prompt. This type of assessment provides the teacher with information and helps determine a student's mastery level. Summative assessment is also the result of a state mandated writing test. Summative assessment may be the last stop, but it is not the last straw. Here are a few examples of summative assessment:

- Scores that are used for accountability for schools (average yearly progress)
- District benchmark or interim assessments
- State mandated assessments
- End of unit tests (for writing, this refers to the end of a unit of study)
- Product/exhibit
- Portfolio review
- Demonstration
- Timed writing
- Published writing

Defining Formative and Summative Assessment: The Garden Analogy

If you think of children as seeds, then *formative assessment* would simply be the watering and feeding of those seeds until they sprout into plants, at which point you would carefully observe those little plants and keep track of their growing process. If the plants look a little limp, you may simply need to provide them with more sun or water. A new setting closer to the sun may be required. Everything you do at this point *affects the growth of these plants.*

Summative assessment would represent admiring the fully grown plants and possibly measuring how tall they have grown. You may analyze their measurements and adjust their care accordingly, but this analysis is not the only link that directly affects the growth of the student. The growth takes place because of the care (formative assessment) that you provide to them during the growing process.

First, take a moment to think about your current practices around assessing writing:

1. Are you skilled in gathering accurate information about students' development as writers?

2. Do you think you use this information to adapt your teaching?

3. Are you assessing throughout the writing process or only at the end of an instructional unit of study?

4. What are some ways you typically assess students' writing in your classroom?

5. Does your assessment guide your instruction?

"We plan. We develop. We deliver. We assess and evaluate the results of the assessment. We revise, deliver the revised material, and assess and evaluate again.
Perfection is always just out of reach; but continually striving for perfection contributes to keeping both our instruction fresh and our interest in teaching piqued."

Palomba & Banta

---

3 Student Self-Assessments That Help Plan Manageable Writing Goals

━━━━━━━━━━━━━━━━━━━━ ✃ ━━━━━━━━━━━━━━━━━━━━

"Study without reflection is a waste of time."

—Confucius

━━━━━━━━━━━━━━━━━━━━ ✃ ━━━━━━━━━━━━━━━━━━━━

In this moment in time, teachers are in the hot seat in America; teacher effectiveness, accountability, merit pay, jobs are tied to test scores, and so on. The discussion is all about how teachers need to do *more*. But when I sit down next to Eddie to talk about his persuasive piece about why sharks shouldn't be feared as much as they are, or listen as Selena reads me her narrative about her baby brother's bad habit of squishing peas in his fingers, all the hounding thoughts about my own efficacy turn into white noise. Side by side with a child, I know I am good. I am going to get that student writer where he or she needs to go, day by day. Because I have the assessment and teaching tools—all the strategies I share in this book—and I have the best secret weapon of all: my students' ability to assess themselves.

In this chapter we look at two vital, often undervalued aspects of teaching writing: self-assessment and its twin, goals-setting, both of which put students in the driver's seat of their own education. These two life skills ensure that when teachers use the gradual release method of handing over responsibility that students are ready and able to catch it, to take the independence handed to them and navigate their own next steps as writers. Building self-assessment into writing workshop gives students opportunities to recognize not only what they have learned but what they need to work on.

I am a self-reflector. I look at each day's lessons and think of what went well and what didn't. It's what makes me grow as a teacher . . . and the same holds true for my students. Throughout this chapter, I use the words self-assessment and reflection synonymously, because to me they are. Reflection has a connotation of thinking about something while assessment implies a more formal written response. Either way, accountability and setting short- or long-term goals is the objective. Student self-assessment plays a key role in encouraging students to evaluate their work at every stage of the writing process or at the end of a unit of study on a particular genre of writing. By setting goals, students do not rate their success simply based on a grade. They have to examine their past performance as writers in more nuanced ways and articulate in words what they will do to develop their writing talent further.

In short, it's a two-way street: teachers need to do all they can to get their writers to perform, and students need to do all they can to make that happen. Frequent, supportive formative assessment by the teacher, paired with students who have been taught how to be self-assessing learners, is what leads to sustained writing achievement. The following quote underscores how vital the student's role is:

> Self-assessment by pupils, far from being a luxury, is in fact an essential component of formative assessment. When anyone is trying to learn, feedback about the effort has three elements: recognition of the desired goal, evidence about present position, and some understanding of a way to close the gap between the two. All three must be understood to some degree by anyone before he or she can take action to improve learning . . . . If formative assessment is to be productive, pupils should be trained in self-assessment so that they can understand the main purposes of their learning and thereby grasp what they need to do to achieve. (Black & William, 1998, p. 143)

My Students' Favorite Self-Assessment Techniques

With any of the strategies that follow, use the four key steps outlined here so students understand the purpose of the self-assessment and have a clear sense of what they are supposed to do;

1. Include student input in defining the criteria that will be used to evaluate their work.

2. Model for students how to apply those criteria to their own writing.

3. Provide concrete feedback to students on the self-assessments.

4. Guide student efforts to develop productive goals and action plans.

Individual Checklists

An individual checklist helps students hone in on their areas of need and work toward improving these areas. A checklist is more short term and often used with many pieces of writing. The teacher may find that it is necessary to help struggling students recognize specific skills based on a particular trait of writing or unit of study. For example, if my class is working on a personal narrative unit of study then certain skills are needed for this type of writing. A few of these genre-specific skills may be

- problem/solution structure,
- plot follows a beginning, middle, end (BME) sequence,
- entertaining beginnings,
- building suspense,
- clear moment in time, or
- create a satisfying ending.

A student checklist based on areas of need would look something like this: I will . . .

____ Grab my reader's attention with an entertaining beginning

____ Focus on a clear moment in time

____ Create suspense in my middle paragraph

Individual student checklists also apply to the revising and editing steps of the process. As the student works on a personal narrative piece this checklist is a handy reminder of the areas that need special attention from the writer. It allows students to give themselves credit for specific areas and each checklist is differentiated based on the needs of each student.

Figure 3.1 on the next page is a student's rough draft. This particular writer re-read her work and thought back on the revising skills I taught her. She created a checklist based on what she felt that her writing needed. Each time she added to or improved her writing based on the skills on this checklist, she put a check on the line. In other words, she gave herself credit for those tasks at hand.

Exit Tickets

What I Have Learned

An exit ticket is a quick and easy way for students to let me know what they have learned in class. I like to use this type of assessment 2 to 3 times a week. It helps to hold the students accountable for their learning. The "I Learned" type tickets are very popular and quick to administer (see Figure 3.2 on page 45).

EXIT TICKET

What I learned today that will make me a better writer:

_____
_____
_____
_____
_____
_____
_____

Figure 3.1   Student Sample: Individual Checklists

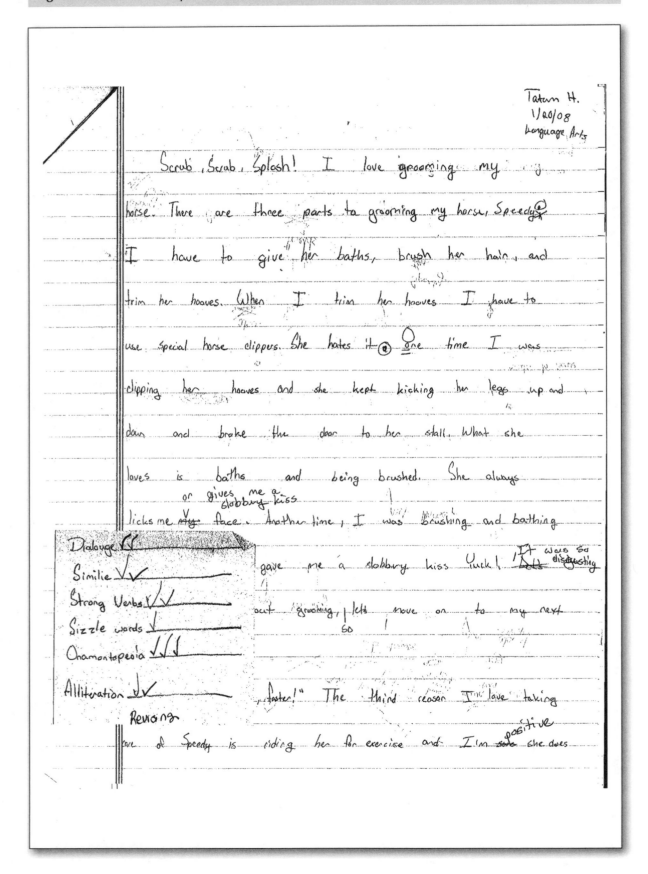

Figure 3.2   Student Sample: What I Have Learned

> **EXIT TICKET**
> What I learned today that will make me a better writer: Today I learned about strong verds. We looked at week verbs (run) & made them stronger (sprinted) This really helped my writing perfect.

What I Needed Help With

This type of exit ticket targets the learning goals that I am trying to get students to recognize (Figure 3.3). This recognition leads to internally controlled motivation and intrinsic motivation. I like to have my students complete this type of self-assessment at least once a week. One variation I provide is that, on the back of the exit ticket, I ask students to give me two ways they can fix those areas of need (Figure 3.4). It is almost like setting a mini-goal.

> **EXIT TICKET**
>
> Areas of writing that I needed help with today are:

Figure 3.3   Student Sample: What I Needed Help With (Front)

> **EXIT TICKET**
> Areas of writing that I needed help with today are:
> I had a hard time organizing my narratives. There were parts that seemed out of order & confusing.

Figure 3.4 Student Sample: What I Needed Help With (Back)

Goals

1. Go back to my B, M, E Plan.
2. Re-read my story.

Journal Entries

This type of self-assessment or reflection can be done in the writer's notebook or in a progress journal. Students can reflect on any problems they are having during or after a lesson. It is important that steps or resources (materials) to fix those problems be included in the entry. Other students can be considered a resource as can materials in the classroom (thesaurus, dictionary, sight-word cards, or student samples).

Self-Created Rubrics (Based on Performance and Effort)

Older students may enjoy creating rubrics for grading purposes, but I usually use a rubric provided to teachers by my school system. I do, however, have my students help me come up with a rubric for their performance in class. One way is with the use of participation cards. The ones in Figure 3.5 are given to each student. These cards are kept in the back of their writer's notebooks, in a library pocket. At the end of a class, or a week of instruction, or even after a published piece, I simply ask my students to rate their performance based on the number scale the cards show. Then I ask them to explain to me how their performance could have improved. This can be done verbally or written in the writer's notebook.

Figure 3.5 Self-Created Rubrics

I didn't do what had to be done and that is why I earned a LEVEL 1.	I did all that I had to do and that is why I earned a LEVEL 2.
I did all that was asked of me and that is why I earned a LEVEL 3.	I did all that was asked and more and that is why I earned a LEVEL 4!!

Open-Ended Questions (aka Sentence Stems)

Throughout a unit of study on a particular genre (narrative, expository, poetry, etc.), I ask my students to reflect on aspects of writing. There are several open-ended questions I use to spark a discussion and then written reflection. This written reflection can be written in notebooks, on sticky notes, index cards, on a goal setting page, and so on. Remember, we want students to evaluate where they have been, how well they performed, what areas need work, and what steps they need to take next. These "next steps" are personal goals.

- Why did I write this piece?
- Where did I get my ideas?
- Was this piece easy or difficult to write? Why?
- What did I learn from my writing?
- What areas do I see I still need to improve?
- How do I plan on improving these areas?
- Did feedback from a teacher or peer help me with my writing? How?
- What elements of writer's craft did I try today?
- Did something I read influence my writing? If so, what?
- Where will I go from here? Will I publish my writing? Share it? Expand it?
- How much effort did I put into my writing today?
- How could I improve my performance today?
- What are the most valuable things I learned today? Why?

ACTION PLANS AND GOAL SETTING

In any tier, student accountability is critical. If students can recognize what they did well, they will repeat it each time they write and the same holds true for weaknesses. If students can recognize an area of weakness and learn a strategy that will help to alleviate this weakness in future writing, then steps are being taken to improve the writing. This is our goal as writing teachers: to show our students how to become independent writers. No one is or ever will be a perfect writer. It is one of those tasks where perfection is strived for but never achieved. As Stephen King says in his writing memoir, *On Writing*, "Only God gets it right the first time." Students can monitor their progress through action plans and goal setting

Action Plans

An action plan is a long-range plan that a student creates based on personal goals. Many of my students who fall into Tier 2 (or 3) lack confidence in writing. A simple recognition of areas of strength and areas of need gives students a closer look at what they are doing effectively and what areas need improvement. At the beginning of the year, I give a basic writing prompt, usually a personal narrative, and ask my students to "show me what they know" about not only the genre of a personal narrative but also the craft of writing as well. I take these writing samples home and evaluate using a basic strengths/weaknesses T-chart. I create a T-chart for each of my students as well as one for each of my four classes. The individual T-charts are needed to help assist students with creating an action plan. The area of *need* found on these individual student T-charts also guide my instruction. As I confer individually with each student, we take a closer look at the strengths and the needs. I ask their opinion about the piece of writing and what they feel good about and what they struggled with. Then I show them my comments on their T-chart. We definitely take time to celebrate the good moments in the writing, but growth comes from extinguishing those areas of need. The areas of improvement are the ones that need to be incorporated into an action plan. From the needs that the *student* notices combined with those *I* notice, we can create an action plan that is individualized and based on specific evidence from the strengths/needs chart (Figure 3.6). The class strengths/needs are discussed further in Chapter 5. In a nutshell, the patterns of problem areas I see help me plan my unit of study and the minilessons that I need to focus on (Figure 3.7).

Figure 3.6 T-chart for Identifying Student Strengths and Needs

Areas of Strengths	Areas of Need

Figure 3.7 Student Action Plan: Template and Example

Student Action Plan

Student Name_____ Teacher_____

Date_____ Grade _____

Areas of Strength:

1. _____

_____

2. _____

_____

Areas of Need:

   1. _____

     _____

   2. _____

     _____

Actions that I will take to improve the areas of need:

   1. _____

     _____

   2. _____

Student Action Plan

Student Name <u>Missy Smith</u> Teacher <u>Ms. Morris</u>

Date <u>9-27-2011</u> Grade <u>4th</u>

Areas of Strength:

   1. <u>I used dialogue in my beginning. "Come on!" My mom yelled. "We have to go to the funeral home."</u>

   2. <u>I like the way that I changed the word "said" to "yelled."</u>

Areas of Need:

   1. <u>When I am going over my paper I need to get rid of so many "ands."</u>

   2. <u>I need to be more specific when I am talking in my story. I am going to add more details.</u>

Actions that I will take to improve the areas of need:

<u>I need to circle all of the "ands" in my paper and stop starting my sentences with the word "and." When I am planning, I need to make sure I have lots of details before I draft.</u>

Goal Setting

So just how do you help students become good at setting attainable goals for their writing? You need to follow the steps above (Figure 3.6) that include modeling for students, and students need to take ownership for recognizing the qualities of good writing, because after all, that's every student's ultimate goal. My students and I call it the learning target (or goal). Students also need to know the criteria (the steps) for reaching it.

To be effective, goals should meet three criteria. They should be meaningful, measurable, and attainable.

Goals help students set priorities and stay motivated. They also help students recognize their strengths in writing and identify areas that need further improvement. While it is my job, as the teacher, to guide my students in their goal making, it is also my role as an effective educator to step aside and acknowledge the importance of independence. Some of my students have never set a goal for themselves, so a little background knowledge on not only the *what and how* we set goals but also the *why* we set them, usually helps them make good choices. I model for my students some of my own goals I have for my writing. I use previously written pieces to determine *what* areas I need to target and work on and *how* I plan to improve these areas. And because I want to continue to have my writing published, I understand *why* I must constantly re-evaluate and learn from my own writing. I show students that keeping goals small and achievable helps me accomplish the goals quickly. Most of my struggling writers think on a more short-term basis rather than a long-term basis. One method my students use for setting goals is the Student Goal Chart (Figure 3.8). This is a long-term goal based on evidence found during timed or published scored writing. The student goal chart allows students to track their individual results over the course of time. My students keep the following prompts in mind when creating goals and action plans:

- My goal is…
- My strategies for reaching my goal are…
- What I need to work on is…

Figure 3.8 Student Goal Chart Template

Student Goal Chart

Name_____

Writing Goal _____

_____

_____

_____

My score at the beginning of the unit of study was at a level_____

My goal is to be at a level_____, _____times by _____

Specific things I need to do while I am revising and editing are:

_____

_____

_____

Date and topic for each writing assignment:

1. _____

2. _____

3. _____

Once students are comfortable with the basics of goal setting, you can give them a form like the one that follows so they have a chance to monitor their experience with goal setting.

Evaluating My Goals and My Results

Please use the following scale to respond to the statements below.

  1: strongly disagree

  2: disagree

  3: neutral

  4: agree

  5: strongly agree

****

_____ 1. Setting goals helped me focus.

_____ 2. Reflecting at the end of each lesson has helped me realize what I need to work on.

_____ 3. We have done an appropriate amount of reflecting.

_____ 4. The reflecting has helped me.

_____ 5. I have been doing well reaching my goals.

_____ 6. My goals are realistic.

_____ 7. Reflecting helped me to improve my writing.

(Continued)

(Continued)

_____ 8. My grades have improved.

_____ 9. I feel like I have been learning more in writing class.

_____10. I feel more in control of my own learning.

Students aren't the only ones with goals. As an educator I must have a clear-cut set of goals in mind for my students. These goals give me a path for success and help guide my planning and instruction.

Goals for My Student Writers

I want every student to:

- Live like a writer, paying close attention to the world—observing, questioning, wondering, having opinions, and seeing other perspectives
- Learn strategies for finding ideas
- Develop a sense of themselves as writers, to reflect on *their* process, and to set goals
- Learn to write with clear intentions and purposes
- Be active members of a writing community, sharing their writing, giving, and receiving
- Appreciate the writing process itself—to possess a willingness to write to discover what they have to say
- Develop a working knowledge of the qualities of good writing
- Create a repertoire of strategies that will lift the quality of their writing
- Become familiar with various genres as containers for writing
- Develop an understanding of the purpose of revision
- Learn to edit using appropriate writing conventions
- Develop strategies for internalizing what is taught in minilessons and conferences
- Develop an understanding that what is learned in the writing workshop applies to *all* the writing they do

I believe that through the implementation of interventions, progress monitoring, and authentic assessment, my students can achieve the goals I have set for them as writers and more importantly, the goals they set for themselves.

4 Monitoring Students' Progress as Writers

━━━━━━━━━━━━━━ ❧❦ ━━━━━━━━━━━━━━

"Without continual growth and progress, such words as improvement, achievement, and success have no meaning."

—Benjamin Franklin

━━━━━━━━━━━━━━ ❧❦ ━━━━━━━━━━━━━━

So let's take a breath and do a recap of how RTI is playing out in the writing workshop. The teaching practices and routines of the writing workshop—minilessons, conferring, small group instruction, sharing, and so on—constitute your Tier 1 teaching, and in the midst of these routines you do a fair amount of informal progress monitoring of your Tier 1 students. The assessment ideas in Chapter 2 provided more deliberate ways of knowing each of your student's writing strengths and needs throughout the year. In Chapter 3 we looked at planning tiered instruction and techniques for student goal setting.

In this chapter we explore some methods that work especially well for Tier 2 and Tier 3 students for whom writing is very hard work. Let's look at Curriculum-Based Measurement (CBM). CBM began in the 1970s with research headed by Stan Deno at the University of Minnesota.

CURRICULUM-BASED MEASUREMENT (CBM)

CBM is an ongoing method of monitoring student progress. It helps teachers determine how their students are progressing and also the effectiveness of the instruction the student is receiving. If a student is below expectations, the teacher changes the form of instruction and the amount of time needed for instruction. This information helps the teacher determine in which tier a child needs to be placed. The benefits of CBM are numerous but a few positive characteristics are that it

- is quick to administer,
- provides efficient and effective feedback,
- uses visual graphs to help teachers, parents, and students see week-by-week progress, and
- motivates students to meet personal goals.

For me, this tool has been a gift for my struggling writers who make progress, not by leaps and bounds, but at a slow, steady pace. By documenting this progress frequently, struggling writers can set very realistic personal goals, achieve them more readily, and feel more empowered to continue their slow and steady progress. If, however, a student is not making progress, I can identify it quickly and make an instructional change.

There are two particular skill areas that I use CBM for: written expression and spelling. I administer them to my entire class early in the year, and then it's only the Tier 2 and Tier 3 level students who are given follow-up tests; Tier 1 students are tested at least two times per grading period.

1. Written Expression

    * Writing fluency
    * Words per minute
    * Free-writes
    * Quick writes

2. Spelling

    * Accurate spelling count
    * Spelling probes
    * Correct letter sequence

Directions for Administering Writing Probes for Written Expression

One of my main goals for my students is to be able to write accurately as well as quickly (rate). This combination of the two goals is their *writing fluency*. The state mandated writing test calls for our students to write on demand, and in Florida's case, in a very short amount of time (45 minutes). It is my job to get them prepared.

Materials needed for a "words per 3 minutes" writing measurement include the following:

- A story starter (I use these when we are working on narratives)
- A quick write topic (I use these when we are working on expository essays)
- Timer (students are given 3 minutes to write)
- Pencils
- Notebook paper
- Folder for each student
- Graphing charts (Figures 4.1, 4.2, and 4.3)
- Running-record keeping chart (for the teacher)

I distribute the notebook paper and pencils. You can write the story starter or the quick write at the top of the notebook paper, but I have 86 students and simply writing it on the board and asking the students to copy the information at the top of their own paper saves time. We always put a name and the date on each test we take. I collect them and place them in individual assessment folders.

The entire process of administering a CBM for writing takes less than 10 minutes. Here is a look into our classroom on a day I am administering a CBM. For this example I am looking at a simple *words per 3 minutes count* (WPM). I will show you an additional example when we get to the *accurate spelling word count* section of this chapter. Here is a sample of the graph (Figure 4.1) I refer to in the scenario below.

Figure 4.1 Words per 3 Minutes Graph (WPM)

	Test 1	Test 2	Test 3	Test 4	Test 5	Test 6	Test 7	Test 8	Test 9	Test 10	Test 11	Test 12
Date												
Date												
Date												
Date												
Date												
Date												
Date												
Date												
Date												
Date												
Date												

Good morning students, I would like to administer a word per minute fluency check today. Please take out your pencils and make sure they are sharpened and ready for writing. Susan, will you please pass out the notebook paper for me? And I will need Ben to pass out the words per minute graph that we use.

Please put your name and the date on the notebook paper and I need you put the date in the next column of the graph for me. Excellent, we are ready to begin. Since we are currently working on expository writing, I will put a quick write topic on the board for you. Please copy what I put on the board at the top of your notebook paper.

Ok, now that all of us are ready, I will give you 2 minutes to think about the topic in your head. (I wait 2 minutes)

Let's get our pencil points ready to write. The quick write topic is Favorite Food. I know you will all do well with this. I am setting the timer for three minutes . . . on your mark, get set, and write!!

At this point I walk around making sure all students are on track. When the timer goes off, I go back to the front of the room.

You did an excellent job today. Please count the number of words you wrote in the three minute time frame. I need you to put this total at the bottom of your notebook paper and circle it. Then I need you to write the word total on your graph (This doesn't take very long for the students to count and record.)

I would like to see thumbs up if you reached our fall goal of 53 words. Please put your thumbs down. Now I would like to see thumbs up if you improved, even by one word, your total number of words count.

This is an example of a graph after several WPM tests have been given (Figure 4.2).

Figure 4.2 Sample Graph

	Test1	Test2	Test3	Test4	Test5	Test6	Test7	Test8	Test9	Test 10	Test 11	Test 12
Date												
Date												
Date												
Date												
Date												
Date												
Date 9-5				60								
Date 8-21			55									
Date 8-17		48										
Date 8-10	45											

I can make a quick formative assessment on how well the class did. I will, obviously, take a closer look at the graphs and document the total results on my running record-keeping chart.

I use the writing fluency norms words per 3 minutes chart that is based on the research of Shapiro (2001) (Figure 4.3). For students who are not at grade level, based on the words per minute norms, I administer more timed WPM tests like the one I outlined for you. Practice makes perfect, and I need to give the struggling students more opportunities. The additional WPM tests can be given in small groups (Tier 2 and Tier 3) and progress monitored. I find that there is a direct correlation between the students who score below grade level on timed summative assessments (state or teacher administered) and the words per minute results. These students are struggling with thinking on demand and their writing stamina is not as developed as it should be. Let's take a moment to distinguish the differences between a WPM measurement and an accurate spelling count (ASC) measurement.

Figure 4.3 Writing Fluency Norms WPM (Shapiro, 2001)

Grade	% Ranks	Fall	Winter	Spring
1	75	7	17	20
	50	4	13	16
	25	3	8	11
2	75	27	33	38
	50	21	25	28
	25	14	18	22
3	75	41	48	50
	50	33	41	42
	25	27	34	33
4	75	53	57	60
	50	45	48	57
	25	36	40	39
5	75	60	65	69
	50	51	55	57
	25	43	45	45

Doing the Words per 3 Minutes Count

CBM writing probes are pretty simple to administer. I use a whole group setting at the beginning of the year to get an overall view of how quickly my students write. I add the component of how accurately they write later on in the year. I need to build up their stamina without too much fear or worry with regard to spelling and punctuation. I want the words on the paper. It is difficult to teach students to write if they have a fear of writing. This is why I start with a WPM measurement; my students think they are fun and the stress level is low. For this type of assessment, my students simply count the number of words they were able to write in a 3 minute time frame. As in the example I shared with you, the students (or the examiner) count up and record the total number of words written during the 3 minute probe. Misspelled words are included in the total. Calculating the total words written is a quick scoring method, but it does only yield a rough estimate of writing fluency. For me, I am ok with this drawback because my goal is stamina and sticking to the topic. Once I see improvement with the abilities of my struggling writers, I add the element of spelling to the probe. This type of measurement is what I refer to as the ASC.

In the box on page 59 are some prompts that will help get you started with the WPM probes. There are prompts everywhere and most teachers have file folders full of them, but the following are ones that I have used in my classroom.

Free-Writes and Quick-Writes

For my struggling writers not only is producing language difficult for them but a "paralysis from analysis" halts their efforts at creativity. Two strategies that have proven to help all of my writers, but especially those who struggle, are free-writes and quick-writes. If you have 10 minutes a day, you can use either of these techniques and make a difference in your students' ability and desire to write. I use the quick-write method when I am assessing for words per minute. I do not use the free-write method for assessment because sometimes the hardest part of writing is thinking about *what* to write *about*.

Free-Writes

Free-writing is simply a stream of consciousness. In other words, it is writing without stopping or analyzing. I call it "emptying the brain" or "clearing the cobwebs." Free-writing releases built-up anxieties that many students have about writing. These anxieties have often derived from low writing scores or lack of understanding of the writing process. The steps to free-writing are pretty simple:

1. Write without stopping for ten minutes

2. Write about whatever you want

Now this sounds simple enough, but it can be a challenge. My goal for a free-write is purely stamina and getting words on paper. Peter Elbow's book *Writing with Power* is an excellent resource for teachers who want to learn more about free-writing. Free-writing is an effective way for students to learn who they are as writers, without judgment. It is all about the process of writing and not the product that guides this strategy. My students are not required to count the number of words or to document results on a chart; this is purely a warm-up and stamina building activity. It is a good idea, before any CBM is administered, with a quick-write that students take the time to work through a few free-writes as practice before the game. No prompts are given and the only supplies needed are pencil and paper.

Quick-Writes

I am a huge fan of quick-writes. It is the writing and thinking on demand that stimulates children's language and helps loosen up the physical ardor of writing. I think of it as a stretch before the big race. There are similarities between quick-writes and free-writes. Both are short, ungraded, and based on process over product. One main difference is that quick-writes are more guided. Typically a prompt-based topic is used to springboard the writing. Another difference is that I build in a sharing time after each quick-write. Because the writing is based on similar topics, sharing serves as a vital tool to see into each other's interpretations and perceptions. I have a set of rules posted in my classroom. They are gentle reminders that it is not perfection that is sought, rather thinking on demand and recording one's thoughts. Here is that chart.

Quick-Writes

- Don't try to write perfectly. Just write what comes to mind.
- Don't erase—simply cross out changes. Just keep writing!
- Change nothing. Do not go back and revise and edit.
- Don't lift your pencil . . . just write and write.
- Remember: The goal is an uninterrupted flow of thoughts.

Expository Prompts for a Quick-write (Use these for practice and the WPM)

1. My accomplishments
2. Favorite movie
3. Why education is important
4. A hobby I have
5. Why I like/dislike animals
6. I wish I could . . .
7. My favorite holiday
8. The best book I ever read
9. Goals I have
10. Favorite weather

Narrative Story Starters (use these for practice and the WPM)

1. The happiest day of my life was when . . .
2. My fondest school memory is . . .
3. Did you know that I can . . . ?
4. The scariest thing that has happened to me is . . .
5. One day I was walking to school and . . .
6. The girl found a toy in the yard that . . .
7. The zookeeper noticed that the cage was open and . . .
8. Last week a dog wandered in my school and . . .
9. I found a note under my pillow that said . . .
10. I was talking to my friends when all of a sudden . . .

Directions for Administering the ASC

I administer an ASC the same way I do a WPM count. The difference is how I evaluate it. Let's take the same scenario as the one I shared earlier but notice the differences in some of the language.

Good morning students, I would like to administer a word per minute fluency check. Today I am also adding the component of accurate spelling. Please take out your pencils and make sure they are sharpened and ready for writing. Susan, will you please pass out the notebook paper for me? And I will need Ben to pass out the word per minute graph that we use. Please put your name and the date on the notebook paper and I need you put the date in the next column of the graph for me.

Excellent, we are ready to begin. Since we are currently working on narrative writing, I will put a story starter prompt on the board for you. Please copy what I put on the board at the top of your notebook paper.

Ok, now that all of us are ready, I will give you 2 minutes to think about the prompt in your head. (I wait 2minutes)

Let's get our pencil points ready to write. The story starter prompt is, "I was on my way home from school and . . ." I know you will all do well with this. I am setting the timer for 3 minutes . . . on your mark, get set, and write!!

At this point I walk around making sure all students are on track. When the timer goes off, I go back to the front of the room.

You did an excellent job today. Please count the number of words you wrote in the 3 minute time frame. I need you to put this total at the bottom of your notebook paper and circle it. Then I need you to write the word total on your graph. (This doesn't take very long for the students to count and record.)

I would like to see thumbs up if you reached our spring goal of 60 words. Please put your thumbs down. Now I would like to see thumbs up if you improved, even by one word, your total number of words count. I will collect your samples, circle any misspelled words you have, and adjust your total number on the graph. You wrote your total number in pencil and I will write the adjusted number in red.

Now I have a chart that reflects accuracy and rate. If the accuracy is an area of need, due to the misspelled words, I need to look a little closer at narrowing down the problem. Let's use the same chart from earlier but look at it with regard to accurate word spelling. In red, I have written the adjusted numbers after I looked over the WPM test, circled words misspelled, and then adjusted the count. Figure 4.4 is what a typical chart would look like after four probes.

A CLOSER LOOK AT SPELLING

Many of my fourth grade students are poor spellers when they come to me. Not only is their recall of how to spell basic sight words low but they aren't equipped with spelling strategies to help them become more successful. I cover a few spelling strategies that I use in Chapter Six.

There are two ways I monitor a student's level and progress with spelling. I have shown you the first way, using a quick-write or story starter. I refer to this method as the ASC. My goal with that type of assessment is to build up the number of words written in 3 minutes. I have found that with timed tests, the more my students practice writing in short spurts, counting the total number of words written, and deducting the misspelled words from their total WPM, there is less stress when the time comes for the state mandated test or in-class summative timed tests.

The second way I assess my student's spelling is with a word list. I refer to the list type assessment as a spelling probe. The goal of the probe is to recognize and count the

Figure 4.4 Sample Graph

	Test 1	Test 2	Test 3	Test 4	Test 5	Test 6	Test 7	Test 8	Test 9	Test 10	Test 11	Test 12
Date												
Date												
Date												
Date												
Date												
Date												
Date 9-5			58 60									
Date 8-21		54 55										
Date 8-17		44 48										
Date 8-10	42 45											

correct letter sequences (CLS). CLS counts pairs of letters that are placed together correctly within a word. This way a student can receive partial credit for words that are not completely spelled correctly. This is important because the words I give to the students have not been taught. The traditional type of spelling tests allow time for students to practice and study, the words on the probe list are referred to as cold . . . much like a cold read, where the text is also unfamiliar to the students.

The Spelling Probe

Spelling probes can be given individually or to a group of students. At the beginning of the year, while I am collecting my baseline data, I give the probes to all students. As soon as I evaluate the assessments and see a pattern as to who is struggling with basic spelling, I begin to give these tests during Tier 2 small group settings. The Exceptional/Special Education (ESE) teacher, who services those students in Tier 3, also gives the probes during small group instruction time.

Where do I Find the Word Lists?

There are a number of sources from which the teacher can build a pool of words:

- Commercial programs
- District grade-level lists
- Basal reading series
- Grade-level vocabulary
- Fry's 300 instant sight word lists

Preparing for the CBM Spelling Probes (Tests)

After the core spelling list has been established, the teacher randomly chooses words from the list. For grades 1 through 3, the list will contain 12 spelling words and for grades 4 through 8 the list includes 17 words. There is also a time frame in which each word is given, based on the grade level. For grades 1 through 3, a new word is announced to the students every 10 seconds. For grades 4 through 8, a new word is announced every 7 seconds. The spelling probe is administered just like the good old fashioned spelling test we have all given. What the teacher does with results, however, is where the difference lies. I think another view inside my classroom would help make this clear.

Students, today we are going to have a spelling probe. This is another word for test, but unlike the tests you are used to, this one will help me help you, individually, with the area of spelling. Jack, can I have you pass out the numbered answer sheets? And I need for everyone to make sure they have a sharpened pencil.

Let me go over the basic rules for the probe:

1. *Listen carefully as I read each word to you.*

2. *Write the first word on the first line, the second word on the second line, and so on.*

3. *You will have 7 seconds to spell each word. (If you are giving this test to grades 1 through 3, you will say 10 seconds.)*

4. *When I go to the next word, write it down, even if you are not finished with the previous word.*

5. *There are 17 words for this probe. (If you are teaching grades 1 through 3, this number will change to 12.*

6. I will say each word twice.

7. If the word is a homonym, I will use the word in a sentence.

At this point a new word is called out every 7 seconds (or 10 seconds). The total time for the test is close to 2 minutes. It is my job to walk around and make sure that that the students are writing on the correct line.

After 2 minutes, please stop and put your pencils down.

The tests are then collected and I score them. I keep all of these tests in individual assessment folders right along with the accurate words count and the words per minute counts.

Supplies Needed for the Probe

- Student's answer sheet
- Word list
- Stopwatch

Here is a sample of the student answer sheet (Figure 4.5).

Figure 4.5 Sample Answer Sheet

Word	Student Spelling	CLS (correct letter sequence)
1.		
2.		
3.		
4.		
5.		
6.		
7.		
8.		
9.		
10.		
11.		
12.		
13.		
14.		
15.		
16.		
17.		

When you compute the CLS for each word, the simplest way is to count up the number of letters and add one to the total. For example, the word book has four letters but the CLS would be 5. Why do you add one? Because the one point that you add is for initial space holders, or in the world of CBM, *phantom letters*. This phantom letter is not considered in the student spelling, only in the word that the teacher calls out. Here are a few other guidelines to keep in mind when calculating a student's CLS:

1. The initial letter of proper nouns must be capitalized. You will notice in the student sample chart that I deducted a point because the Letter M in the word Monday was not capitalized. The word *Monday* has a CLS of 7, but the student spelled the word monday so the student CLS is 6.

2. Internal punctuation (apostrophes, hyphens) in words is counted as a point. An example would be *won't*. The CLS for this word is 6. If a student leaves out the apostrophe, then the student CLS would be 4.

3. If a word has double letters, and a student provides one of those double letters, then a point is given. Here is an example: The CLS for *putting* is 8. If a student's spells the word *puting* their CLS point total is 6.

4. Any letters omitted will affect the CLS. A basic example of this would be the word *sprain*. The CLS is 7 but if a student spelled it *spran*, the student CLS would be 5.

5. Any extra letters added to the spelling of a word also affects the CLS. An example of this would be *preass*. The correct spelling is *press* and has a CLS of 6. The way the student spelled the word the student CLS is 5.

Now here is a sample of an actual students' answer sheet (Figure 4.6).

Figure 4.6 CLS Student Sample

Word + 1 for phantom letter	Student Spelling (students receive credit for any correct letter)	CLS (correct letter sequence)/ SCLS (student CLS)
train 5+1=6	tran (credit for *t-r-a-n*)	6/4
dress 5+1=6	dreass (credit for *d-r-e-s-s* but subtracted for the *a*)	6/5
yellow 6+1=7	yelow (credit for *y-e-l-o-w*)	7/5
pretty	purty	7/4
Saturday	saturday	9/8
press	preass	6/5
sprain	spran	7/5
because	because	8/8*
kitten	kiten	7/5
tomorrow	tomorow	9/7
please	pleese	7/5
airplane	airplane	9/9*
small	small	6/6*
money	muney	6/4
water	water	6/6*
color	colur	6/4

CLS score: 112

SCLS score: 90

*Total Words Spelled Correctly: 4

Where Do I Go From Here?

At this point you have given the spelling probe and added up the possible CLS points and the student's CLS points. It is easy to count the number of words spelled correctly, however, the most important task is to determine the CLS. Also, note that if a student spells all of the words correctly, there is no reason to determine the CLS score. If a student misses just a few words, go back and look for patterns in the misspelled words.

Based on the research of Shapiro (2001), if a student earns less than one-half of the total possible CLS then a spelling probe from a lower grade will need to be used. This would be an indicator that most of the words were spelled incorrectly. But again, it is the CLS we want to look at. The CLS should show patterns, and these patterns can help teachers with their curriculum.

The previous student sample shows, even though most words are not spelled correctly, that this particular list of words is an appropriate place to start for this student because of the CLS score, we don't want our students at a frustration level, just like with reading. The concept is the same. When choosing a just right book we count the miscues within a student's oral reading and determine if the book is too hard, too easy, or just right. The same with the spelling probes. This is an excellent differentiation tool for not only the struggling writers placed in Tier 2, but for our gifted and on grade-level students who need to be challenged.

Let's look at the student sample in Figure 4.6. I can determine that:

1. Only 4 words were spelled correctly.

2. The SCSL score is 22 points away from the CLS score. Since this is not at the 50% mark of inaccuracy, the words from the list give me place to start.

3. The patterns I see with the words spelled incorrectly and the SCLS column shows me that this student has difficulty with consonant vowel consonant (CVC) patterns in spelling and with doubling consonant rules. This gives me a place to start with my spelling instruction.

Let me clarify that I do not give 86 individualized spelling tests once I have completed the probe. Out of my 86 students, I had a total of 10 who needed a lower level word list because the SCLS was 50 percent (or more) of the CLS. I had a total of 6 approaching grade-level students who, like the student sample earlier, needed direct instruction based on spelling patterns, but the original list I used was a good place to start. I serviced the 6 approaching students and the ESE teacher serviced the 10 below grade-level, or Tier 3 students. I administer a spelling probe two times a month for my group of students and the ESE teacher gives a spelling probe one time a week. I do not give additional spelling tests. The spelling probes make spelling individualized not cookie cutter. As for the on-grade-level and advanced spellers, I focus on their spelling, not through probes or old-fashioned tests but through their writing.

FOUR STRATEGIES FOR DEVELOPING WRITING FLUENCY

Writing fluency is the natural flow and organization of written work. It is easier and more enjoyable to read a piece that is organized and makes sense. Many of my struggling writers struggle with fluency. My two goals for fluency, as stated earlier in this chapter, are accuracy and rate. I have shown how quick criteria-based measurement can help teachers keep track of their students' progress. My goal with CBM is not to dissect every word a student writes. The spelling probes are a guide for differentiating and analytically assessing the needs of students. I need to know them in order to teach them. I am never more focused on the curriculum and the assessment than I am the learner. By engaging our students with a variety of writing assessments and writing opportunities we, as teachers, can finally feel like we have a grasp on how and what to teach. I would like to offer some additional strategies that will help build fluency but do not require a graph, a prompt, or a worksheet. These additional writing opportunities can be delivered in a minilesson or in addition to a minilesson. These strategies work well at the beginning of the year to help build an understanding of sentence construction and stamina as well as to build a community of writers who share their work. But don't dismiss using these strategies during small group instruction.

1. **Start with a sentence**. Begin with the concept of a sentence and build from there. I remember when a teacher came to me after a workshop very concerned about the progress of her students. She had the "bottom of the bottom" struggling writers and desperately wanted to know where to start. I told her to start at the beginning. A student can't write a paragraph or a full-blown story if the thought of writing a simple sentence is intimidating and a struggle. She smiled and asked if I was serious! I smiled back and said I was. I asked her to go back to her class and focus on helping her students write the best sentences they could. She did, and she was thrilled with the results. We do have time to slow down. And when we do, we learn about our students on an intimate level that lets them trust us and lets us reach them.

2. **Next, focus on paragraph organization**. Model ways to vary sentence beginnings and length for your students. A simple slinky has helped my students "see" the sentence length while I read a mentor text, picture book, or a student sample of writing. I give each student a small slinky and as I read, they stretch out the slinky based on the length of the sentence. If it's a short sentence, the slinky stretches just a little and for the longer sentences, the slinky stretches out really long. When my students read their own stories as part of the revising process, we focus on fluency, and it's the neatest scene to see your students all stretching and evaluating the lengths of their sentences.

3. **Have students read their work aloud**. Doing so helps them check the fluency of their work, allowing them to hear the natural flow of their sentences and ideas. I have a basket of whisper phones that students can use if they are reading their piece to themselves. If a student hears choppiness? He or she highlights the section so he or she can go back and revise it. Students can also read aloud to a partner

4. **Provide immediate feedback to your students**. Children need feedback as they're writing a piece to keep them motivated and heading in a good direction. A brief conference of just a few minutes can do wonders to support a writer. I also show my students how to form writing groups and sharing circles. For our sharing circles, I draw a large circle on the white board. As a student either finishes his or her writing for the day or needs assistance, he or she writes his or her name inside the circle. As another student reaches the same point as the first student, his or her name is written underneath the first name and a writing partnership is established. These two students

find a quiet spot in the classroom and share their writing. The goal of this type of sharing is feedback, and the students really enjoy it. A writing group is the same concept except this group is usually made up of three to four students. The quality of the feedback is important too. I like to provide students with a few phrases to use when complimenting writing and also some constructive language that improves the writing and supports the writer rather than deflating him or her.

Constructive Ways to Compliment Writing:

- I like the way your story (essay) began because . . .
- My favorite was when . . .
- I like the way you explained . . .
- I liked the words you used in your writing such as . . .
- I like how you used dialogue to make the story sound real.
- I liked the details you used to describe . . .
- I like the way the story ended because . . .

Constructive Questions and Suggestions to Improve Writing:

- Could you add more to this part about . . .
- Do you think your order would make more sense if you . . .
- I got confused in the part about . . .
- Could you write a beginning sentence that catches your readers?
- Could you use a better word for _____?
- I think that if you add_____(simile, alliteration, onomatopoeia) it will add creativity to your piece.

USING CBM TO WRITE RTI GOALS

CBM scores from the initial screenings are easily translated into goals for RTI intervention. Using CBM to write goals lets teachers accurately compare performance early in the year to later in the year (and throughout). The test administration and scoring are consistent and quick. A desirable goal for the WPM probe is to achieve a score at or above the 50th percentile (Shapiro, 2001). Students who fall below the 25th percentile are considered at risk and possibly considered for Tier 3. These students are monitored more frequently to recognize growth with writing stamina. The students who perform between the 25th and 50th percentile need the strategic intervention that Tier 2 provides and will also be monitored, just less often.

Any goal set for a student, based on the CBM findings should be:

1. For a specific time period—usually

2. Specific—easy for a student to understand

3. Measurable—in other words, the goal can't be something vague like "write more often" or "likes to write" because you can't measure these goals with an assessment

I keep all records, charts, quick-writes, anecdotal notes, and so on in individual assessment folders.

A CLOSER LOOK AT PROGRESS MONITORING

Progress monitoring involves ongoing data collection on specific skills that are important for student success. It is a formative assessment that provides accountability and evidence for RTI services. Progress monitoring is an integral part of RTI. Students are exposed to high quality interventions, monitored through CBM, and only considered eligible for ESE (Exceptional/Special Education) when no response to interventions has been determined. The main goal to remember here is: Teachers must collect formal and informal data about their students' needs and their progress. This data must drive the instruction. By monitoring the progress of our students, the rates of improvement, and identifying those students who are not demonstrating adequate progress, teachers can catch struggling students who need either strategic or intensive instruction before they fall so far behind. With the subject of writing, it would be disappointing to find out that 50 percent of my students did not understand how to organize an expository essay only after a test was given. Or even worse that a large percentage of my students were unable to show proficiency on the state mandated writing test, again, only after the results were posted. There is a lot of back tracking that would need to done to correct the confusion. If, however, I had monitored the students step by step throughout the writing process, many mistakes and confusion could have been corrected and identified much sooner. This is where I believe a good bit of time is wasted . . . going back.

There are some distinct differences between progress monitoring and traditional assessment. There is a place for both in the classroom. In my experience, the more CBM that I use, the more feedback that I give, and the closer I monitor my students and adapt my instruction, the better my traditional (summative) scores are. It is a win-win situation.

Progress Monitoring: Formative

- Conducted frequently (twice per week for students with disabilities, once per week for those at risk, and monthly for those average or high achieving students)
- Quick and easy method for gathering data (simple charts like the CLS or WPM examples as well as folders of student examples)
- Analysis of student progress helps to modify instruction (it is about recognizing areas of need and providing strategic instruction to those who need it)
- Student goals can be adjusted

Traditional Assessments: Summative

- Typically lengthy
- Administered infrequently (once per quarter or after a lengthy unit of study)
- Teachers and students do not receive immediate feedback
- Opportunities to modify instruction are limited (the test is over so the instructional objectives change)

The No Child Left Behind Act requires all schools to show Adequate Yearly Progress (AYP) towards the proficiency goal. CBM can be an effective tool to fulfill the AYP evaluation in written expression and spelling. The measures are simple and easy as well as reliable. By tracking and monitoring our students, we can prescriptively teach what needs to be taught. RTI is a framework that gives instructors a chance to reach unresponsive students and provide the necessary tools and strategies for growth. Teaching writing is hard. But by distinguishing between what needs to be taught and what has already been learned, as well as what is working and what is not, our jobs actually become easier and our students become more proficient writers.

5 Strategies That Transform Struggling and Reluctant Writers

∾∽

"There is not another academic skill that demands that a child bring together as many different neuro-developmental functions as are required for writing."

Dr. Mel Levine

∾∽

Writing is hard. Teaching writing is harder. Most teachers will tell you that one of the most difficult skills to teach is writing. I know several teachers who avoid teaching writing as much as they possibly can because they are not comfortable with the multitude of skills that must be taught. And many students feel that to write a story or an essay is a painstaking process.

In this chapter, I zero in on the specific challenges of students who get lumped under the umbrella term *struggling writer*. In previous chapters, I provided strategies for tiered instruction that addressed the needs of struggling writers. Now, let's look at what, in particular, makes composing hard for these students.

ATTRIBUTES OF THE STRUGGLING WRITER

I find that most struggling writers come to me with underdeveloped skills in these areas:

- Motivation to write
- Understanding of the steps of the writing process
- Organization, planning, and revising

- Ability to self-select strategies to help accomplish writing tasks
- Knowledge of topics and background knowledge to draw upon
- Knowledge of what makes a piece of writing effective
- Grade-level spelling and basic conventions
- Ability to self-regulate and become an independent writer
- Confidence in ability to write

Many of the students that I teach live in poverty, speak English as a second language, and have learning disabilities. Add to these difficulties the stress of high-stakes testing for writing and you have a recipe for too many children having the deck stacked against them. As teachers, even without doing extensive assessment, you know pretty early on in the school year which students need you the most. The bottom line? Get to these kids first, get to these kids often. They need intensive, individualized, and explicit teaching of skills and strategies within the first weeks of school. By taking a few extra steps, we can lessen the dramatic range of abilities in a typical classroom setting. I would even go so far as to say that the intervention strategies in this chapter and throughout the book can transform the lives of many of these struggling writers.

Make Purposes for Writing Crystal Clear and Highly Engaging

Students need to write routinely for real purposes, and they need teachers to constantly show them samples of real-world writing. Book reviews, newspaper stories, editorials, samples of writing from the local community, and so on. Get students writing to persuade others about topics that matter to them, from changes they want at school to changes they wish to see in their community. We need to dispel the assumption that writing is only a school skill or something you learn to pass a test. At the beginning of the year I create a large anchor chart called *Purposes for Writing*. Here is a sample anchor chart.

Purposes for Writing

- To tell stories
- To make people laugh and cry
- To share experiences
- To express our emotions and make sense of our experiences
- To express our point of view
- To record and retell events
- To write notes
- To write letters, emails, and blogs
- To persuade
- To label
- To fill out forms
- To interact and communicate with others
- To give directions
- To document learning
- To explain and teach

All of these purposes for writing are connected to one of the most important traits we teach: voice. When my struggling students find that voice within themselves their confidence comes across their face like a blush. It's astounding how suddenly they can love writing. It is that critical moment when they realize, "What I have to say is important." Let's take a closer look at the connection between understanding author's purpose and finding of voice in writing.

Lessons on Author's Purpose and Voice

Immerse yourself in both fiction and nonfiction picture books in order to discover the authors and books that your instincts tell you will resonate most with your children. Mentor text lessons during which you read aloud and invite students to surmise why an author wrote a particular book are so powerful for struggling writers. Go online and find author interviews you can share. Look at Patricia Pollaco's books because there is so much autobiographical passion. Read the about the author paragraphs on book jackets because they often have insights as to what inspires the writer to write. Funny books? The purpose may be purely to entertain and make readers laugh. Memoirs? To keep family heritage alive (Think *Grandfather's Journey* by Allen Say, Cynthia Rylant's *When I Was Young and in the Mountains*). Great nonfiction picture books like *Owen & Mzee*, written by a father-daughter team and a zoo director, prove to writers that nonfiction can be full of emotion and make you cry, and that there can be several purposes for writing any genre. This particular story is about a young hippo and a tortoise who bonded after a tsunami in 2004. The authors wanted to stir emotions in others about this remarkable animal friendship and also educate people about the need to fund wildlife organizations all over the world.

Do lots and lots of reading and talking together over many days before you even ask students to try think about their own writing ideas. They need many examples in order to develop a deep, nuanced understanding that writers who have a strong connection to their material often are those whose books have the most noteworthy voice. Create an anchor chart on which you keep a running list of ideas about voice:

"It's like talking speech written down."

"The author's heart is in it, you can tell."

"I can hear the author is from the South. I can hear the southern accent!"

"I can always tell Kevin Henke's books because it just sounds like him."

"William Steig always uses funny fancy words!" Confer and watch your struggling writers with an eye and an ear for whether a fiction or nonfiction genre captures their attention most of all. By parading lots and lots of examples in front of them, students begin to see their options for writing and they are more likely to find a groove, deliberately and subconsciously borrowing format ideas and tone from the published books they've heard, and by gosh, their own voice emerges!

For fiction, here are some picture books that have worked especially well in helping students hear the voice of the author and character:

- *Dear Mrs. LaRue: Letters from Obedience School* by Mark Teague (a pleading voice)
- *Diary of a Worm* by Doreen Cronin (a worm's perspective on life)
- *Math Curse* by Jon Scieszka (a funny/comedic voice)
- *The Spider and the Fly* by Mary Botham Howitt (a compare/contrast voice between two characters)
- *My Many Colored Days* by Dr. Seuss (a range of emotions)

Find your own unique ways for helping your struggling writers get concepts through nonwriting avenues, such as role play, acting out a scene, or art. For example, after reading the book *My Many Colored Days*, I provide each child with a box of crayons and their writer's notebooks. We explore how colors can represent emotions. I ask students to complete the following sentence stems:

- If frustrated were a color, it would be . . . because . . . some examples from my life are . . .
- If happy were a color it would be . . . because . . . some examples from my life are . . .
- If nervous were a color it would be . . . because . . . some examples from my life are . . .
- If confident were a color it would be . . . because . . . some examples from my life are . . .

The stems can be about any color. Notice that this activity can be used for two purposes:

1. To recognize emotions and how they affect voice

2. To collect moments from their lives that represents these emotions . . . in other words, collecting ideas to write about, which is part of the next component of voice, choice

Choice Enriches Voice

Another critical component of voice is choice. Think about it, those published authors became well known because there was something very special about the words upon each page and the story they added up to. That something special was a strong bond between the authors and their topics and ideas. And it is strong and full of voice because these writers *chose* the topic and *chose* to do all the dreaming and writing and ample revision and living through rejection letters that no doubt went on before the book was published. I look closely at providing students choice in writing in Chapter 6. Donald Graves (1983) eloquently states, "When voice is strong, writing improves, along with the skills that help improve writing." The links to voice are purpose and choice. I like to provide all of my students a chart that includes the mnemonic device for the various purposes writers write (see Figure 5.1).

Again, when struggling or reluctant writers find their voices, they also discover their confidence as writers. But I can't overstate this point—give it time. I have found that if I slow down and focus on the depth of my lessons and not just coverage, I am laying down a foundation that can be built upon. If you think you can cover something in one day and it takes three, that's okay! That is why the writer's workshop works so well for all writers. The brief minilesson (10–15 minutes) is concise and manageable. Then the independent writing time (50 percent of your class time for writing) is when students have that precious *time* to practice what you taught them. And finally, the sharing part of writer's workshop (10–15 minutes) provides students with the opportunity to share with the group and learn from each other.

Figure 5.1

Author's Purpose: PIES

P: persuade
I: inform
E:entertain
S: show emotions

THE WRITING PROCESS

One of the main issues I find with my struggling writers is the lack of knowledge of the writing process. While conducting workshops for my district, I have found that many teachers are unfamiliar with the writing process. I typically get many blank stares when I ask, "How many of you use a writing process when teaching students how to write?" This explains why many students are unfamiliar as well. For a student who is proficient with writing, the process is important, but for my lower level students, it is critical.

All students need quality instruction in order to be successful writers but the struggling writers need to know all of the nooks and crannies of the process and strategies for each step of the process. In Chapter 6 I breakdown the writing process and provide strategies for each step. The basic writing process is compiled of the following five steps: prewriting, drafting, revising, editing, and publishing. One note of caution on the writing process, there is not *one* linear process. I share with students a five-step model from Pulitzer Prize-winning journalist and teacher, Donald Murray. He identified these steps after observing how thousands of writers, both student and adult, organize their thoughts and actually write. He feared that naming steps would create rigidity, and alas, it has. Many classrooms that I have visited have this very process posted for their students as if there is a single, linear writing process. The writing process is recursive and all students will not be at the same step at the exact same time, and that is ok. The flexibility that the writing process offers is ideal for RTI and in Chapter 6, I show the connection between the writing workshop (and the process) and implementing RTI.

What Makes the Writing Process Difficult for Some Struggling Writers

Figure 5.2 shows some of the difficulties students have with each step of the writing process. I am not including publishing because I do not find too many students who need help with this step. Publishing is actually the step most writers (of all levels) love the most.

Just about any student who struggles with writing can benefit from adaptations. Even my students who are successful writers benefit from the adaptations, especially if creating a particular genre of writing (narrative, memoir, expository, poetry, etc.) is more difficult than others.

Adaptations for Writing

Whole-class, one-size-fits-all approaches to writing will never meet the needs of struggling writers. These writers need adaptations to be successful. Adaptations do not last forever. They should be selected based on the needs of struggling writers and implemented accordingly. Most students require only accommodations while some have such a deficit with writing that they may need significant changes in teacher

Figure 5.2 Problem/Accommodation Chart

Step of the Process	Problem	Possible Solution
Prewriting-planning	1. Choosing a topic 2. Narrowing down a topic 3. Limited details 4. Little knowledge of sequence of events 5. Little knowledge of writing genres	1. Use hand mapping strategy 2. Inverted triangle method 3. Use the W5+H1 method 4. Sequencing ladder 5. Reading many different types of writing *Solutions 1-4 are elaborated on further in Chapter 6.*
Drafting	1. Difficulty beginning a piece of writing 2. Transitions are usually "then" or "next" 3. Repeatedly stops during drafting (worried about conventions) 4. Difficulty organizing their ideas 5. Little understanding of author's purpose	1. Student adds to details of planning page or talks out the story with the teacher 2. Provide a chart of alternative transitions for the writer's notebook or writing folder. 3. Provide pencils without erasers to help the student see that mistakes are ok. 4. Show the storm and sort strategy 5. Minilesson on Persuade, Inform, Educate, Entertain, Show Emotion (PIEES)
Revising	1. Limited vocabulary 2. Lacks knowledge of creativity skills (alliteration, onomatopoeia, etc.) 3. Most sentences start with "I" hurting sentence fluency 4. Unsure of reasons to revise or steps 5. Limited knowledge of how to add, change, rearrange, or delete details	Revising is a critical part of the process of writing. When students are revising my minilessons focus on these areas as well as the others that are found in Chapter 6. I typically spend 3 days, after a rough draft is written, showing students how to fix up their piece of writing. To me, 90 percent of writing is the rewriting. This is where the heart of teaching writing craft lies.
Editing	1. Unable to identify spelling errors 2. Little knowledge of grammatical rules 3. Unclear about how to edit	1. Model how reading a story backwards (bottom to top and right to left) helps a writer see errors. 2. The grammar pages from the reading series offers many helpful lessons. 3. Provide a Capitalization, Usage, Punctuation, Spelling (CUPS) chart for reference. Also a simple chart of proofreading marks is helpful.

expectations. These students are the ones who fall into the Tier 3 category and are served by our Exceptional/Special Education (ESE) specialist. It is my Tier 2 students who benefit from the following accommodations.

Accommodations in Environment

- Increased instructional time for writing (based on the results of the Words per Minute [WPM] from Chapter 3). I typically pull my struggling writers for small group intervention during independent writing time
- Quiet workspace
- Work with an occupational therapist

Accommodations in Materials

- Simple prompts (example: Tell about a time that you were happy or sad and write a story about it.)
- Simple graphic organizers or checklists
- Individualized spelling lists (based on the Accurate Spelling Count (ASC) from Chapter 3)
- Personal copies of alphabet strips

Accommodations in Strategies

- Reteach skills in a small group setting
- Use peer tutoring to reinforce the skill or strategy taught
- Provide additional homework opportunities at home
- Show students how to set attainable goals (example: Instead of correcting all of the misspelled words in a draft, a struggling writer may only be required to correct half of them.)

Students who struggle with writing will need to see the teacher model a strategy 3–4 times before they may feel comfortable and successful using it.

A Few More Suggestions

As teachers of writing, we provide numerous types of assistance on a daily basis. But typically we teach using the whole-group instruction model. With RTI, a strategy

---

Peer Tutoring

Peer tutoring is a method of instruction that involves students teaching other students. It is a win-win situation. First, if a student can teach another student, then the level of mastery is reached. So for the advanced or proficient writers, this serves as a way to increase their own level of knowledge. For the struggling writer, there is a level of comfort between peers that is often not as formal as the one they may see with the teacher. I have found that a one-on-one situation works best for peer tutoring. It is also important that both students understand the goal of the tutoring session. I model the process in the whole-group setting several times before the students engage in the process. I also vary the roles of the students during the tutoring session. I ask that my proficient writer help a struggling writer on one or two areas of need. I set the times for roughly 10 minutes. Then, I reverse the roles and ask the struggling writer to help the proficient writer with a compliment or a question or some helpful advice. My goal is for all students to benefit from the process.

---

or minilesson is still introduced whole group, but then small groups are formed (based on formative assessment and observation) and differentiated instruction takes place within those small groups. For students who struggle with writing, accommodations in the learning environment, instructional materials, and teaching strategies will need to be put into play. I want a choice in my accommodations because we all know that what works for one student may not work with another. This section is a compilation of ideas and accommodations that have been helpful to my struggling writers. I look at these accommodations on an individual needs basis. Sometimes a small change can make a big difference. You may choose to use the suggestions as written or modify according to a student's particular need or your grade-level expectations. I am categorizing the possible problems in the following ways: spatial relationship, tactile/fine motor, stamina, environmental, and organizational (see Figure 5.3). Later in this chapter, the teaching approach of differentiated instruction is covered in depth. This approach focuses on student interests, learning styles, and environment.

Figure 5.3 Problem/Possible Solution Chart

Problem	Possible Solution
Environmental	For the student who finds the conventional desk top inflexible, the use of a padded lap desk can provide the varied angles the students may need.
Environmental	Allow a student to experiment with different writing spots in the classroom. This may include a table, lying on the floor, or maybe standing.
Environmental	Some students require a quiet setting to write. Provide head phones for any student that may be easily distracted by conversations between other students.
Environmental	Students who have a difficult time getting started with their writing for the day sometimes benefit from background music. It is important that the music has a steady beat.
Spatial Relationship	To provide a student with indications of where to start and stop their writing, make a green dot for the desired place to start and a red dot for where they should stop.
Spatial Relationship	If a student has difficulty with spatial relationships between words, teach them how to use a popsicle stick or their finger as a spacer between the words.
Spatial Relationship	If a student has a difficult time with left to right progression, place a smiley sticker on the left side of the paper as a visual cue.
Spatial Relationship	To insure proper positioning of the paper, place a strip of masking tape on the desk to show where the outside position of the paper should be.
Spatial Relationship	The use of specialized paper with either raised or colored lines can offer a greater visual contrast and physical boundaries for the student.
Spatial Relationship	Emphasizing the writing line with red helps students see where they are supposed to write.
Spatial Relationship	Tape student's writing paper to their desk at the appropriate slant to keep the paper stationary and free of movement.
Spatial Relationship	If a student has a difficult time with understanding where to start and stop their writing, draw a red line down the right side of their paper and a green line down the left side of their paper to indicate the start and stop lines.
Tactile	Explore different pencil grips to help the student increase control over the writing tool. The use of a grip may also decrease the amount of pressure and effort a student may be using when writing.
Tactile	If a student has a weak grip then allow them to use a felt tip pen or soft lead pencil to write. This helps the student make more discernible marks on the paper with less pressure.
Tactile	Allow the student to have flexibility with the type of writing that is required. Many students are more successful with cursive rather than print.
Tactile	Placing a student's paper on a desktop easel or a slant board helps reduce some writing difficulties by improving the wrist posture. These devices also bring the paper closer to eye-level. An economical slant board is a simple 3 inch binder.
Stamina	Certain written assignments can be orally dictated to the teacher or to another student to be transcribed.
Stamina	If a student fatigues while writing, assess how long the student can write before becoming legibly impaired. Then set realistic goals for the length of writing time. An assignment may need to be completed in 2 days rather than one.
Stamina	Keeping in mind the goal of the assignment, it is usually possible to reduce the amount of written work required or provide additional time to complete the writing task.
Organization	For those students who have difficulty writing their draft on every other line, show them how to set up their draft paper by placing a dot or an x on every other line. The student always writes on the line with either the dot or the x.

Problem	Possible Solution
Organization	Checklists can be made for a student who has difficulty organizing, revising, or editing a piece of writing. These checklists can be laminated for multiple uses.
Organization	Mnemonic devices help many students see multiple steps in process. CUPS (is often used to remind students of steps for editing.
Organization	Graphic organizers are useful tools for students who have difficulty sequencing events in a story or sorting details into paragraphs.

A few months ago, I was searching the web for ideas and I came across two samples of lined paper that can help a student with spatial relationship. I use the crayon method as mentioned in the chart above, but I have found that there are several students I am teaching this year that need a more confined style of paper. Here are the two samples I found (Figure 5.4 and Figure 5.5).

Figure 5.4 Handwriting Paper Sample 1

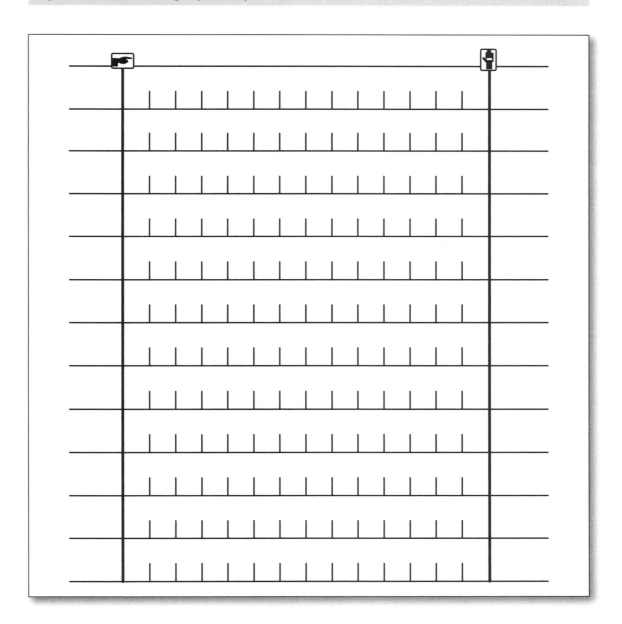

Figure 5.5 Handwriting Paper Sample 2

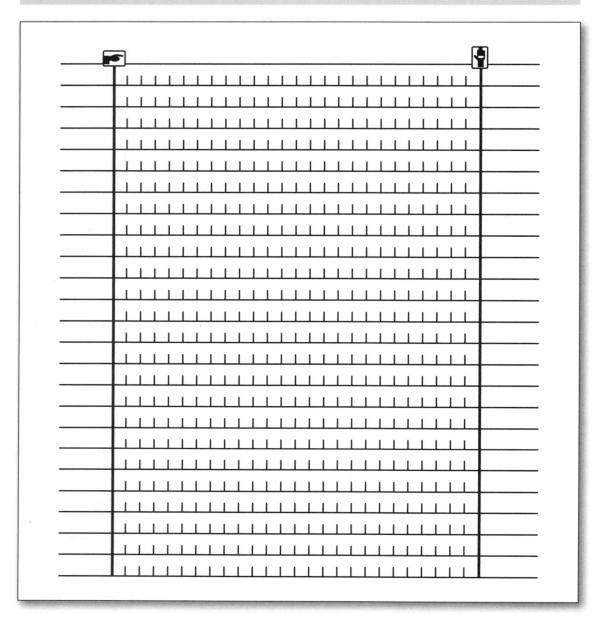

Handwriting

Let's face it, handwriting is important and handwriting issues must be addressed. In our worlds of busy, busy, busy, this skill is often neglected. I am not suggesting that a long period of time is spent on handwriting each day, but some time should be. Many of my struggling writers also struggle to write legibly. I would like to offer a few additional interventions strategies for handwriting that I know work to improve legibility:

- Use a colored file folder that the student can place on their paper so that only one line at a time shows.

- Use yarn, string, or pipe cleaners as boundary markers on paper. The yarn strategy has proven to really work for many of my students. I keep a small basket of precut yarn in the writing supplies area and if a student needs to get a piece of yarn, that is fine. The students simply lay the yarn on the margins of their paper for a visual as to where to stop and start.
- Use golf pencils if a student has an inefficient grasp. This smaller size provides the student with a more efficient grip of the pencil
- Use rubber grip shelf-liners desk tops to help reduce papers from sliding around.

As always, practice makes close to perfect so dedicating a small amount of time daily or weekly to the skill of handwriting is beneficial. Believe me the reader will thank you for it.

DEVELOPMENTAL STAGES OF WRITING

There are six stages of development that are beneficial when addressing the needs of students.

I feel that it is important to show how the stages correlate with the scoring and the tiers (Figure 5.6).

Figure 5.6 How Stages Correlate With Scoring and Tiers

Stage	Score	Possible Tier
Emerging	U/1.0	3
Developing	2.0	2
Focusing	3.0	2
Experimenting	4.0	1
Engaging	5.0	1
Extending	6.0	1

I consider the students in my classroom, who are in the focusing and experimenting stages to be approaching or on grade level. The higher achieving writers fall in the engaging and extending stages. And my struggling writers are those in the emerging and developing stage. I do not attach an age with these stages, but I have read research that does. Instead I attach the ability that I see through anecdotal notes and formative and summative assessment.

Stages of Writing

Stage 1: Emergent Writer

- Little or no topic development, few details
- Little or no organization

- Little awareness of audience, little voice noted
- Errors in surface features prevent the reader from understanding the writer's message

Stage 2: Developing Writer

- Topic beginning to be developed
- Details are listed rather than developed
- Writing shows the beginning of an organized plan
- Transitions may be lacking
- Limited awareness of audience, voice is evident but inconsistent
- Simple word choice
- Simple word patterns
- Errors in surface features (mechanics) interfere with communication

Stage 3: Focusing Writer

- Topic is clear even though development is incomplete
- Evidence of planning is apparent although ideas are loosely organized
- Sense of audience
- Minimal variety of vocabulary, higher-level word choice attempted
- Minimal variety of sentence patterns
- Errors in surface features interrupt the flow of communication
- Transitions apparent and variation attempted

Stage 4: Experimenting Writer

- Topic clear and developed, even though parts are uneven
- Details are relevant and clear in sequence
- Clear plan of a beginning, middle, and end
- Written for an audience
- Voice is evident and effective
- Experiments with language and sentence patterns
- Word combinations and word choice may be novel
- Errors in surface features may interrupt the flow of communication
- Limited amount of text, less developed at the climax

Stage 5: Engaging Writer

- Topic well developed
- Clear beginning, middle, and end
- Engages the reader
- Effective use of varied language and sentence patterns
- Errors in surface features do not interfere with meaning
- Writer's voice is clear
- Related ideas are grouped together and connected with transitions
- Awareness of audience is sufficient
- The text is long enough to demonstrate effective writing skills

Stage 6: Extending Writer

- Topic fully elaborated with rich details
- Organization moves the reader through the piece
- Sustains the reader's interest
- Creative use of creative language
- Varied sentence patterns add flow and rhythm to the writing
- Varied transitional elements connect the like ideas
- The writer's voice is apparent and appropriate
- The test is of sufficient length to demonstrate writing skills that exceed the standards

DIFFERENTIATED INSTRUCTION

Differentiated instruction (DI) is a process and approach to help teachers help students by matching student characteristics to instruction and assessment. It allows all students access to the same classroom curriculum but incorporates a variety of strategies. Differentiated instruction is based upon the belief that students learn best when they make connections between the curriculum and their diverse interests and experiences. Differentiated instruction is not solely for the struggling writer but for the gifted one as well as those on grade level.

Many times I found that I taught writing to the middle. RTI is a mandate but not a learning model exactly. Differentiated instruction is the process by which you accomplish the goals of RTI. I revisited the theory of differentiated instruction and incorporated the two. I certainly don't create individual lessons for each of the students in my class and I don't water down the curriculum for my struggling writer, but I do focus on layering my curriculum for writing within Tier 1 with differentiated instruction. I find that many of my struggling writers make greater gains when their interests become part of the equation. Before I get too involved in the differentiated theory and practice of DI, let's look at a step-by-step plan of action using much of the information covered in the previous chapters.

Step 1: Get to Know Your Students

The first few weeks of school I provide each student with the interest inventory found in Chapter 1. It is important that teachers know the likes and dislikes of their students. It is during this time that I also give my students a learning style inventory. No child makes use of just one learning style, but nevertheless, teachers can look for preferences. The basic learning styles are presented in Figure 5.7.

Typically your school guidance counselor can give you an inventory that is age and grade level appropriate for your students. This is a wonderful time to send home a parent letter regarding differentiated instruction as well as any RTI information from Chapter 1 that can assist parents with helping their child at home. After a teacher knows the interests and learning style of their students, it is important that he or she begins observing students and recording observations. This is a critical time for

Figure 5.7 Learning Styles

Visual Learners: learn best using visualization techniques	Auditory Learners: learn best by listening and talking	Kinesthetic Learners: learn best by doing
• Pictures • Videos • Diagrams, graphs, charts • Mind maps • Highlighting and color-coding • Colorful maps • Graphic organizers • Lists • Flashcards	• Listening carefully • Recording short notes • Rhyme and rhythm • Memory aids (mnemonic devices) • Talking aloud • Need verbal repetition • Reading out loud • Using whisper phones	• Hands-on activities • Illustrating work • Quick sketches • Constructing drawings • Mind maps • Movement while learning • Manipulatives • Role plays

anecdotal notes as well. Any information that has been discovered through Step 1 should go into an assessment folder. I use one folder per child in my classroom and store them in a hanging file folder crate. I have four classes of writing and 86 to 100 students each year, so this concept will work well with departmentalized as well as self-contained classrooms.

Note of Caution

Despite having a preference for a particular learning style, students are able to learn through other sensory styles. Students should be made aware of their most and less favored styles and learn to adapt to their strengths as well as weaknesses.

If I Ran the School Interest Inventory

One way I like to get to know the interests of my students is through the "If I ran the school" inventory. It is a simple procedure, and I love anything simple. I ask my students to circle 10 of the items on the list that, if they ran the school, they would choose to learn about. I collect these forms and tally up the choices to see what my students would like to learn and write about.

Step 2: Assess Your Students (Formative)

This is all about the formative assessment that was covered in Chapter 2. I typically start the year with a unit of study on a personal narrative. I need to assess what my students already know and what I need to teach. I provide a prompt and the testing conditions of my state mandated writing test (FCAT) and collect the papers. I use the strengths/weaknesses T-chart discussed in Chapters 1 and 2 (Figure 1.3 and Figure 2.1) to document my findings. I create a strengths/weaknesses chart for *each one of my students*. This is the analytical part of my assessment. These individual charts help with goal setting, action plans, and individual checklists. Once I see what my individual students know or need help with, I begin to look holistically at the charts. Patterns begin to surface, both good and not so good, and I need to recognize both. The weaknesses I find and record on the class T-chart are my instruction and I base my curriculum on the areas of weakness that I see need to be taught. It is also important that I look at the scores on the individual papers and assess proficiency levels. It is about prescriptive planning.

Knowing the abilities of individual students and providing assistance and accommodations from the level a student is at is an important factor for RTI. I use the RTI Assessment Chart (Figure 2.2) to record all of my findings. It is also during this time that I am administering the free-writes and eventually I move to the WPM quick-writes. I must model for my students how to use the WPM graph found in Chapter 3 (Figure 3.1). Not too long after the WPM assessments, follow the correct letter sequence (CLS). Remember that the WPM measures written expression, the ASC measures spelling within a words per minute probe. The CLS also measures spelling but for individual spelling lists.

Step 3: Begin the Unit of Study

Let me stop here for just a moment and review the basics for a unit of study. A unit of study is an in-depth study of different writing genres. Typically a unit of study lasts 4 to 6 weeks. Here are a few of the genres that I teach throughout the year:

- Personal narrative
- Expository essays
- Poetry
- Memoirs
- Feature articles
- Persuasive papers

Now it is time to start working through the writing process. Data has been collected from several sources and lessons have been created based on the needs of the students. I believe that you will find Chapter 6 a valuable resource because it breaks down the writing process and provides strategies for each step of the process. As the unit of study begins, my small group RTI instruction begins. Instead of acting as an assistant, the speech teacher is now serving as an additional instructor for my students. I find that planning (the step of prewriting) is difficult for my struggling writers, so I keep a close eye on the students who I noticed have unorganized or underdeveloped papers from the pre-assessment. Again, I know this information because of the pre-assessment that I gave and the recorded information on the RTI Assessment Chart (Figure 2.2). It is important that conferring and anecdotal notes based on observations, are recorded. Remember that with anecdotal notes, I have a chart for each student. This makes it convenient when I want to file these notes in a student's personal assessment folder. It is important that the weekly WPM, CLS, and ASC are being administered on a needs basis, during small RTI group instruction. As you continue to teach the unit of study, model for your students a few formative assessment strategies from Chapter 2 (fist of five, yes/no cards, thumbs up/thumbs down, I learned statements, etc.). And finally it is time for students to publish their personal narrative and for the teacher to score the papers for proficiency. I score these papers using the state rubric that our school system provides.

Step 4: Asses Your Students (Summative)

After I have taught a personal narrative (or any genre) going step by step through the process, I administer a timed test of the same genre using the procedure outlined by my state writing test. I also use the rubric that is used for the state or countywide test. I pre-assessed with this method and post-assessed with the same method. The pre-assessment serves as a formative assessment and the post-assessment serves as a summative assessment.

I am also, once again, creating the strengths/weaknesses T-charts for individual students as well as a whole class T-chart (I have four classes, so I create a class T-chart for each group of students). My students look over their writing goal from the beginning of the year and self-assess if they met this goal. A new writing goal is written based on the weaknesses found on the new strengths/weaknesses T-chart. All of this information is stored in the individual assessment folder. The whole class T-charts are used to help me plan my next cycle for the same genre (personal narrative). I typically work through a unit of study for two cycles before introducing a new genre to my students. Here is a framework for my first few units of studies.

- Pre-assess with a personal narrative prompt: 1 day
- Unit of study on a personal narrative (student choice-no prompts): 3 weeks
- Post-assess with a personal narrative prompt: 1 day
- Cycle Two: Unit of study on a personal narrative (student choice-no prompts): 2 weeks (the second cycle takes less time than the first one)
- Post-assess with a personal narrative prompt: 1 day
- Pre-assess with an expository prompt: 1 day
- Unit of study on an expository essay (student choice-no prompts): 3 weeks
- Post-assess with an expository essay prompt: 1 day
- Cycle Two: Unit of study on an expository essay (student choice-no prompts): 2 weeks

And the units of study continue following the same pattern. This is just a framework, but it helps to look at long-range planning and then plot your assessments as well as your RTI schedule for instruction. It is about putting all of the pieces of the learning puzzle together.

Step 5: Differentiate Instruction

The rest of this chapter will give you important information based on who, when, why, and how to differentiate instruction. I work through the first cycle of a unit of study before I gradually begin to start differentiating my instruction. Many times I find that the area I differentiate the most is with the process. Because writing is so process-based, and so much teaching time is spent in these five steps, it is natural to focus much of the differentiation in this area.

What Does Differentiation Look Like for Writing?

Teachers can differentiate their writing instruction in three curricular areas:

1. **Content:** Content refers to what we want our students to learn (standards or objectives) and the materials or mechanisms through which that is accomplished.

2. **Process:** Process refers to how students learn (the activities, strategies, or adaptations used to assist the learning).

3. **Product:** Product is the way a student shows what he has learned—something he has *produced*.

Teachers can differentiate according to student's characteristics of readiness, interest, and learning profile. Within the learning profile fits the category of environment. Figure 5.3 addresses many strategies and adaptations that will fit within the three main characteristics I refer to as RIP:

- Student **readiness** (skill profile and developmental stage of writing)
- **Interest** (interest inventories)
- Learning **profile** (learning style and grouping preference)

A Sample of Differentiated Writing Strategies

- Learning/writing contacts (Figure 5.8)
- Varied homework
- Writing groups (based on interest)
- Writing centers (based on interest)
- Jigsaw activities
- Varied graphic organizers
- Choice of writing topics
- Tiered products
- Small-group instruction
- Varied journal prompts
- Writing menus (Figure 5.9)
- Tic-tac-toe (Figure 5.10)
- Tiered Activity (Figure 5.11)
- Independent study of choice topics

The following tiered cone will help you see where and how differentiated instruction fits within the RTI model. Remember, I only use differentiated instruction to enhance my Tier 1 teaching.

Samples of Differentiated Writing Strategies

Figure 5.8 Learning Contract #1

Name_____

My question or topic is:_____

_____

_____

To find out about my question or topic…

I will read:_____

I will look and listen to:_____

I will write:_____

I will draw:_____

I will need:_____

Here is how I will share what I know:_____

I will finish by this date:_____

Figure 5.9 Diner Menu-Writing

Appetizer (Everyone Shares)

- Write a book review for your favorite book.

Entrée (Select One)

- Make a list of onomatopoeia words. Then write a poem using as many words as you can.
- Look through the headlines of a newspaper. Select 20 interesting words and put them in ABC order.
- Create a rap that explains what happens during the writing process.

Side Dishes (Select at Least Two)

- Write an expository essay about your favorite television show.
- Write a class play. You will need a minimum of 5 characters. In the play, include the problem, solution, and lesson learned.
- Write a 5 day journal entry from the point of view of a book character.
- Write a how-to essay about a chore you have to do at home. Make sure the reader understands and could follow the steps taken to complete the chore.

Dessert (Optional)

- Design a birthday invitation, making sure to include important information and special instructions.

Figure 5.10 Tic-Tac-Toe Book Report

Draw a picture of the main character.	Perform a play that shows the conclusion of a story.	Write a song about one of the main events.
Write a poem about two main events in the story.	Make a poster that shows the order of events in the story.	Dress up as your character and perform a speech telling who you are.
Create a diagram comparing and contrasting the introduction and conclusion of a story.	Write two paragraphs about the main character.	Write two paragraphs about the setting.

Figure 5.11 Tiered Activity-Writing a Persuasive Essay: Grades 4th–6th

	Beginning	**Intermediate**	**Advanced**
Outcome/ Objective	Students will determine a topic and will write a five-sentence paragraph with a main idea, three supporting sentences, and a concluding sentence.	Students will determine a topic, state a point of view, and write two paragraphs defending that point of view.	Students will determine a topic, state a point of view and write an essay of at least five paragraphs that uses multiple sources to defend that point of view.
Instruction/ Activity	Students will receive a model of a five-sentence paragraph and explicit instruction in constructing the paragraph. As a prewriting activity, students will list their topic and develop a list of at least three things that support their topic.	Students will receive a model of a persuasive essay and a graphic organizer that explains the construction of a persuasive essay. Students will also receive explicit instruction in writing a persuasive essay. As a prewriting activity students will use the graphic organizer to plan their writing.	Students will review the graphic organizer for a persuasive essay. Students will be given explicit instruction in locating sources and quotes for their essays. As a prewriting activity, students will use the graphic organizer to organize their essay. Students will also compile a list of five sources that defend their main point.
Assessment	Students will be able to write a five-sentence paragraph that successfully states and supports a main idea. The paragraph will meet the criteria on the state writing rubric.	Students will be able to state a point of view and successfully defend the idea using two paragraphs that defend the point of view using main idea and details. The paragraphs will meet the criteria on the state writing rubric.	Students will be able to write a five-paragraph essay that states a point of view, defends the point of view, and uses resources to support the point of view. The essay will meet the criteria on the state writing rubric.

Adaptations for Content

- Devote more instructional time for teaching mechanics
- Reteach writing skills and strategies
- Help students set goals for the writing process (using an organizer before they draft or adjective checklist for adding higher-level word choice)
- Assign homework designed to reinforce writing skills
- Use peer tutors to reinforce teaching instruction

Adaptations for Process

- Simplify writing prompts
- Provide a choice of prompt (still based on the same unit of study)
- Choice of graphic organizers (after several have been modeled by teacher and used by students)
- Individual checklists
- Personal spelling lists
- Provide personal accommodations from Figure 5.3

Adaptations for Product

- Increase amount of time for completing written assignments
- Decrease the length of written assignments
- Reduce or eliminate copying demands
- Evaluate spelling using the CLS rather than the number of words misspelled
- Permit students to use spell checker software
- Grade assignments based on improvement rather than performance
- Allow students to use invented spelling
- Provide feedback on targeted skills rather than all skills

Examples of Feedback

- I like the way your story (essay) began because . . .
- My favorite was when . . .
- I like the way you explained . . .
- I liked the words you used in your writing such as . . .
- I like how you used dialogue to make the story sound real.
- I liked the details you used to describe . . .
- I like the way the story ended because . . .

A Community of Teachers

There is no reason to go alone into the world of differentiated instruction and RTI. Teachers need to work together. RTI and DI are only as good as the teachers who come together collaboratively to create lessons, apply strategies, and share data (both formative and summative). It's no longer a view of my students" but "all students." When the RTI team meets, teachers engage in discussions about not only how well students are performing but what needs to be done for those that aren't. This is where differentiated instruction fits in. Once a teacher knows what her students need, through assessment, she needs a plan of action. I call it a "buffet of ideas." The whole promise of DI is that one size *does not* fit all. So teachers need choices. These choices come in the form of strategies, student choice, and student interests.

It is important that teachers don't look at RTI and DI as different approaches; look at them as a combined effort that meets the needs of all learners. RTI and DI make the perfect team. They have identical goals (to maximize student growth and success) but different origins.

Differentiated instruction emerged as a fully developed model in 1995 (Tomlinson, 1999). The goal was, and still is, to provide many avenues for students to acquire *content*, to *process* information, and to develop *products*.

RTI was originally developed as a better way of identifying students with learning difficulties. The traditional formula for identifying students often waited for students to fall far behind and possibly fail in order to receive the services they needed. RTI identifies struggling students early and provides tiers of support based on the assessments. RTI incorporates frequent progress monitoring and tiers (levels) into the approach. Differentiated instruction is what is used to support these tiers and the strategies are divided into the avenues of content, process, and product. The strategies in this chapter fit nicely into this buffet of options.

The following is a checklist that teachers can use, as a team, to better prepare differentiated lessons.

Ready, Set, Go: Team Planning

Making It Happen
Team Planning

READY. . .

☐ Identify the subjects or concepts that most need to be differentiated based on past experience.
☐ Set professional goals for implementing differentiated instruction.
☐ Gather information about each student's interests and learning profile.
☐ Gather, review, and analyze information about each student's readiness/achievement.
☐ Identify the core knowledge, skills, processes, and products.
☐ Align lessons to the learning standards.
☐ Increase focus on higher order thinking through questioning, assignments, and assessment.
☐ Incorporate structured choice into student assignments or projects.
☐ Participate in a teacher's team to support professional growth.
☐ Discuss differentiated instruction strategies as part of team collaboration.
☐ Discuss the rationale for differentiated instruction with students.
☐ Make use of "differentiated instruction" resources in textbooks and curriculum resources.
☐ Receive informal feedback/encouragement on use of differentiated instruction.

SET. . .

☐ Review routine classroom tasks and modify them to make them meaningful.

☐ Use pre-assessments to determine student readiness for units, skills, or concepts.

☐ Provide minilessons for students who struggle with a skill or concept.

☐ Identify lessons and activities that should be tiered.

☐ Plan and implement a tiered lesson.

☐ Reflect on successes and failures. Share with teacher's team.

☐ Work with colleagues to plan a differentiated unit.

GO!!!

☐ Redesign the classroom to support differentiated instruction.

☐ Work with colleagues to do a task analysis of difficult skills.

☐ Plan differentiated lessons, activities and units to address breakdowns in skills.

☐ Do classroom visits within critical teachers groups. Discuss strengths and needs.

☐ Investigate ways to scaffold student skills so that each tier of instruction becomes more rigorous.

☐ Engage students in self-assessment. Provide coaching to help students differentiate for themselves.

GETTING PARENTS INVOLVED

A major concern for parents, as well as teachers, is how to help children who are having difficulty in school. We need parents to also be our partners and open communication is the hallmark of effective home-school collaboration. The following questions are ones that I have heard parents ask at general meetings or questions that parents have asked me personally. Having a newsletter that goes home at the beginning of the year addressing not only these questions but those that may be generated at your school after an initial *All about RTI* meeting, can help alleviate any concerns that may arise among parents whose children are receiving Tier 2 and 3 services. Because each school and district addresses the avenues of RTI differently, no two newsletters will be alike. In my school, our parent's guide the information we put into the newsletter, and a new one is written each year because the questions change as more parents become aware of the process and terminology of RTI. When parents are made aware of the whole process and then are notified that their child is in need of intervention, they know that this means extra help for their child.

1. How will parents be included in the implementation of RTI and reviewing curriculum options?

2. Does the curriculum offer materials that parents can use at home?

3. Does the school/district have a plan on how to keep parents involved and informed?

4. Are there written materials for parents to explain the RTI process?

5. How will teachers be trained in using tools and methods as supported by research?

6. Are there sufficient resources (time, staff, funding, and materials) to be able to meet the diverse needs of the students in Tiers 2 and 3?

7. What role does RTI play in special education?

8. How do school personnel check to be sure that the interventions are being carried out as planned?

9. At what point in the RTI process do parents have the right to request an evaluation for special education eligibility?

10. What length of time is recommended for an intervention before progress is monitored?

Key Terms Parents Should Know

Response to Intervention (RTI): The RTI model is a multi-tiered approach to providing high quality instruction and intervention matched to student needs.

Universal Screening: The administration of an assessment to all students in the classroom, grade, school, or district.

Student Progress Monitoring: The administration of an assessment to some students in the classroom, school, grade, or district.

Research-Based Instruction: An instructional program or collection of practices tested and shown to have a record of success. That is, reliable, trustworthy, and valid evidence indicates that when that program or set of practices is used, children can be expected to make adequate gains.

If we are going to ask that our parents be active in the RTI process and their child's educational future, we need to make sure we provide them with necessary tools. Many of the parents of my students haven't even thought about writing since they were in school. So the task of helping their child at home may be daunting for some parents. I like to give the parents a few tricks of the trade that serve as a guide for helping at home. Many of my parents appreciate the information.

Activities to Play at Home for Writing Development

Many times I find that my parents are more comfortable helping their child with writing if a little bit of fun is added to the at-home instruction. Here are a few of the activities that my students and parents enjoy the most.

Materials Needed:

- Pencil
- Paper
- Dice
- Magazines
- Crayons
- Timer

Steps for Going over Your Child's Writing at Home

1. Have your child read their writing out loud to you.

2. Verbally respond to the piece of writing.

   "You really knew a lot about your topic."

   "What a great story!"

   "Hearing what you read made me think about . . . "

3. Help your child think through the content of their writing by asking questions.

   "How do you feel about your writing?"
   "Can you show me your best example of word choice?"
   "Is there anything you need to add or take out?"
   "Are you happy with your conclusion?"

4. Guide them through the editing process.

   "Let's read one sentence at a time and focus on how each sentence sounds separately."
   "Let's check the first word of each sentence and make sure it begins with a capital letter."
   "Touch the end of each sentence and make sure you have included ending punctuation."

5. Always praise your child for what they have attempted and accomplished.

Instructions:

   Activity One: Hold a written conversation. Set a timer for no more than 10 minutes. Tell your child there must be no talking while the timer runs. Instead, write down the conversation starting with a question your child can answer. The sillier the questions, the more fun you can have with this activity.

   Activity Two: Create a joke book. Fold pieces of construction paper in half and let your child write one joke per page. This lets them use creative thinking and experience the book making process.

   Activity Three: Cut out magazine pictures and spread them out on a table. Have your child pick one or two pictures. If they choose one picture, they must write a story about that picture. If they choose two pictures, they must write a story that combines elements from both pictures. Determine the number of sentences they must write before they start writing.

   Activity Four: Purchase a pair of dice and use them for creative writing. Think of a story title. Roll one die and the number rolled is how many words you must write. The next person rolls and writes. Keep rolling and writing until your story is finished. Increase the challenge by rolling both dice and adding the numbers together to practice writing longer sentences.

   Activity Five: Make lists that involve creative thinking. Write down questions your child can answer with at least five responses. Set a timer for 10 minutes and both you and your child write down a list of answers. Some questions you can ask are: How would I spend 50 dollars? If I could fly, where would I go? What are some things I would do as president?

A Poem to Share with Parents

Whose Child Is This?

"Whose child is this?" I asked one day
Seeing a little one out at play.
"Mine", said the parent with a tender smile
"Mine to keep a little while.
To bathe his hands and comb his hair,
To tell him what he is to wear,
To prepare him that he may always be good,
And each day do the things he should".

"Whose child is this?" I asked again,
As the door opened and someone came in.
"Mine", said the teacher with the same tender smile.
"Mine, to keep just for a little while.
To teach him how to be gentle and kind,
To train and direct his dear little mind,
To help him live by every rule,
And get the best he can from school".

"Whose child is this?" I asked once more,
Just as the little one entered the door.
"Ours", said the parent and the teacher as they smiled.
And each took the hand of the little child.
"Ours to love and train together.
Ours this blessed task forever."
Author Unknown

I find that parents are pretty receptive to how teachers teach their child and the methods that are used to bridge the ability gap if they are informed and asked to become involved in the education of their child.

However, let's face it, there are some parents who will never become involved in the educational needs of their child or are fired up at the beginning of the year only to lose interest by December. I can't control those factors, but I can feel comfortable in my efforts to include parents. We, as educators, can't force them to want to participate. I love the tried and true quote "You can lead a horse to water but you can't make him drink." I can rest my head on my pillow each night knowing that I offered and requested the support from parents, and I am thrilled with those who are eager to be a team but can only pick up the pieces from those parents that choose not to become involved. The following is a sample letter that can be sent home to parents at the beginning of the year to inform them of the qualities of differentiated instruction.

Dear Parent/Guardian:

Welcome to another great year at _____!

This year, we have three goals as we teach your child. Our first goal is to teach your child the information, skills, and concepts he or she will need to be successful this year based on the standards. We will do this in a variety of ways to ensure that your child is successful. Our second goal is to help all students develop as critical thinkers. In addition to learning the information presented, your child will be expected to apply his or her skills and think about the ideas presented. Our final goal is to start where your child is and help him or her to grow throughout the school year. All students should leave ___ grade with more knowledge, skills, and experiences than they have today.

In order to meet these three goals, we will strive to get to know your child over the next few weeks and throughout the year. We will talk with your child about his or her interests and the ways in which he or she learns best. We will use assignments, pretests, and other methods to learn about the skills your child has mastered and the skills he or she needs to practice. We will use this information to help plan instruction.

Because students have a wide variety of strengths and needs, at times students will complete different learning tasks, assignments, and projects even though they are all learning the same skill. This is known as differentiated instruction. When necessary, your child will receive extra support on assignments. At other times, we will make an effort to provide extra challenge for your child. By doing so, we will help your child continue to learn and grow.

You can help your child succeed by encouraging him or her to be responsible to learn the information, skills, and concepts presented, to demonstrate his or her learning through class work and homework, to strive to get better and better, and to respect others as they do the same. If you have any questions as the year gets underway, please feel free to contact us.

We are looking forward to a great year!

Sincerely,

_____

Differentiated Instruction Resources

Websites to Explore

- Enhance Learning with Technology: Differentiated Instruction
  http://members.shaw.ca/priscillatheroux/differentiating.html

- SDE: Differentiated Instruction Resources
  http://www.sde.com/di/index.asp

- Teachers Network: Adjust Your Teaching Style to Your Students' Learning Styles
  http://.teachersnet work.org/ntol/howto/adjust/

- Technology: The Difference in Differentiation
  http://www.riley.d21.k12.il.us/Resources/tech_differentiation.html

- Technology: How to Differentiate Instruction
  http://www.teach-nology.com/tutorials/teaching/differentiate/planning/

6 Strategies That Support the Phases of the Writing Process

"Nulla dies sine linea" or "never a day without a line"

—Donald Murray

In this final chapter, we look at core teaching strategies that help students better understand the writing process itself. Even though composing is more of a circular process than a straight line, children, especially those that struggle with writing, need to see writing as a manageable series of steps. As students mature and become more experienced, they intuitively see its recursiveness. They know that writers sometimes dive in without a plan or brainstorm, revise during first draft, and make all sorts of idiosyncratic decisions. But I think we do our elementary students a disservice if we don't first let them write with the training wheels of Murray's five stages. And I think we do ourselves a disservice if in a quest to be uber writing teachers, we try to run a workshop with 25 children starting and finishing pieces at different times. It is just too hard for most teachers to manage.

All of my students are not always on the exact stage of the process at the exact same time, but they are pretty close. This enables me and the RTI team to look closely at the students who are below proficiency, identify just what aspects of writing are challenging, and quickly intervene. We pull from a big tool box of strategies—all of the ones I've discussed in this book—and if one doesn't work, we try another, and another, until the writer leaps over the particular hurdle.

In addition to these targeted interventions from the previous chapters, I share many of these strategies for each stage of the writing process with the entire class. All writers benefit from this exposure to a wider array to choose from.

I generally introduce them in minilessons and then revisit them during small group differentiation through Tiers 2 and 3. I use the basic 6-step writing process that Donald M. Murray first described in 1982:

1. Prewriting (collecting ideas)
2. Planning (planning falls into prewriting, but because it is such a major step to prewriting, I usually put it into its own category)
3. Drafting
4. Revising
5. Editing
6. Publishing

As I said earlier, planning and revising tend to pose the greatest challenge, so let's start with planning. And remember, for all these strategies, model how to use the strategy, then give students an opportunity to cooperatively practice the strategy, and finally let students practice independently on their individual papers. As with any subject, writing requires extensive and explicit feedback. The more our students walk the walk of writers and talk the talk of writers, the more confident they become in their abilities.

PREWRITING

"If you breathe, if you live; you have something to write about."

—Donald Graves

Listing

Excellent for: Generating Ideas

Many writers keep lists. I know I do. Lists can be on anything: favorite books or movies (great for writing reviews), happy or sad moments (good for narratives), and lists of favorite words (an excellent tool for revising for word choice). Listing facts is one of the best ways to brainstorm about a subject that interests you (a fantastic way to prepare for expository writing). I ask my students to create lists of potential writing ideas, (Figure 6.1), in their writer's notebooks, so that I never have to hear those dreaded words, "I have nothing to write about." I always try to tie in a good mentor text that can help spark self-connection. These connections are what help our students become collectors of ideas. It is also important that I show my students examples from previous year's lessons. The opportunity to see how other students collected and organized their lists provides reinforcement to students. For struggling writers, visuals reduce apprehension and increase a positive attitude. It is interesting to observe how some students' bullet each entry on the list; some number them, while others simply skip lines between each idea. The goal is to generate ideas for writing. The format my students choose is a personal choice.

Figure 6.1 Listing Example

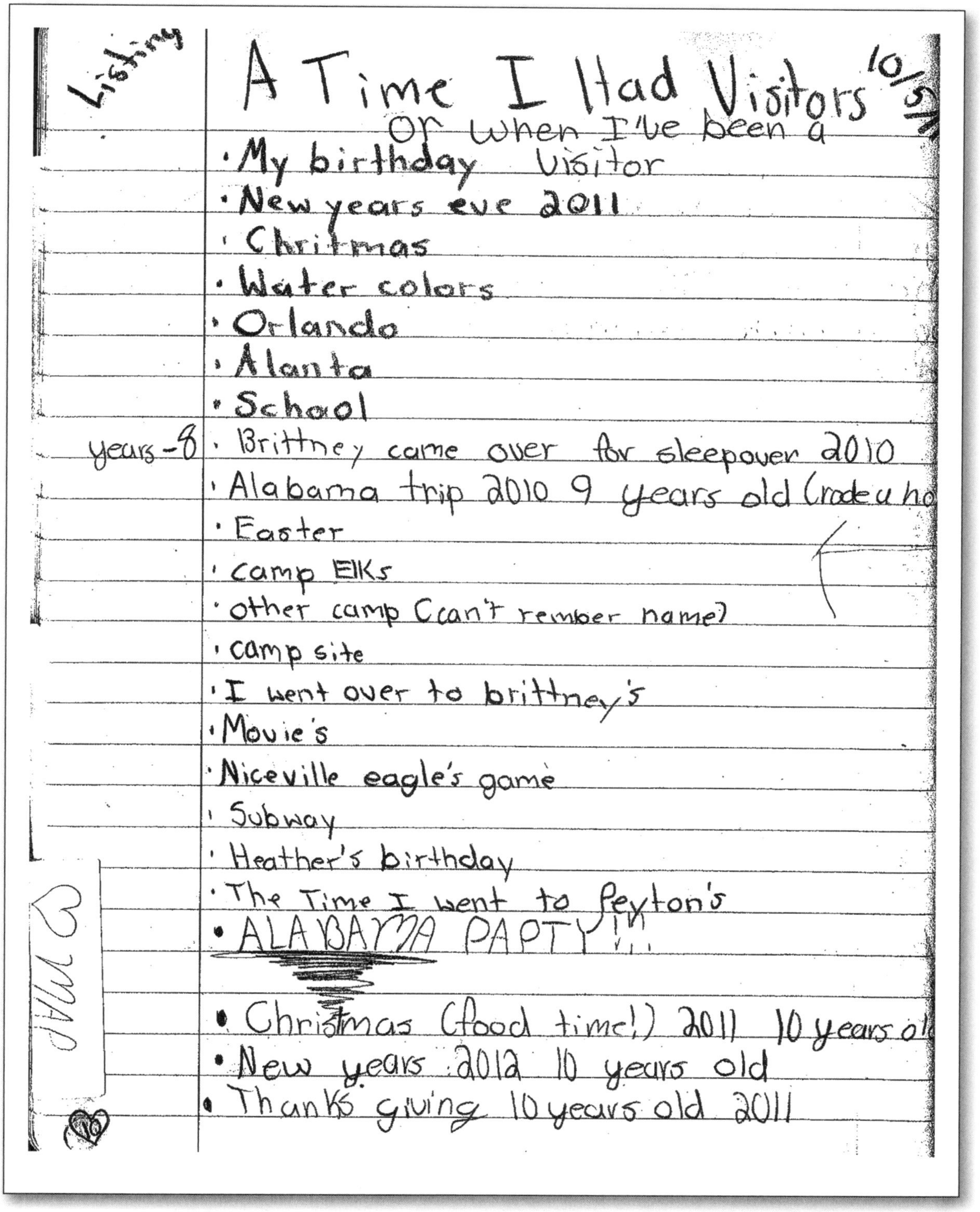

Listing

A Time I Had Visitors 10/5

or when I've been a
- My birthday   visitor
- New years eve 2011
- Chritmas
- Water colors
- Orlando
- Alanta
- School

years–8
- Brittney came over for sleepover 2010
- Alabama trip 2010 9 years old (rode u ho
- Easter
- Camp Elks
- other camp (can't rember name)
- camp site
- I went over to brittney's
- Movie's
- Niceville eagle's game
- Subway
- Heather's birthday
- The Time I went to Peyton's
- ALABAMA PAPTY!!!

- Christmas (food time!) 2011 10 years ol
- New years 2012 10 years old
- Thanks giving 10 years old 2011

Webbing

Excellent for: Generating Ideas and Planning

This is a classic way to plan for a piece of writing. Many students are very comfortable brainstorming with a web. It is quick and fairly simple, and that makes it a favorite. To create a web, students draw a circle in the middle of their planning page (Figure 6.2). The subject they are brainstorming is written in the center of the circle. For example, let's say I just finished reading *Owl Moon* by Jane Yolen. This book is about a child spending time with her father. I may ask my students to write the words *"special times with my family"* in the center of their circle. At that point, I allow students enough time to empty their brains of every self-connection they can think of that is related to the subject word(s) written in the middle. In this case, those subject words are *"special times with my family."* These connections are written outside the center of the web using spokes that connect the memory to the circle. I like my students to take this basic web a step further. Because webs hold an unorganized structure of ideas or details for a selected idea, I show my students how to sort the information they just webbed. I cover this sorting of information more in the planning stage of the process.

Figure 6.2 Webbing Example

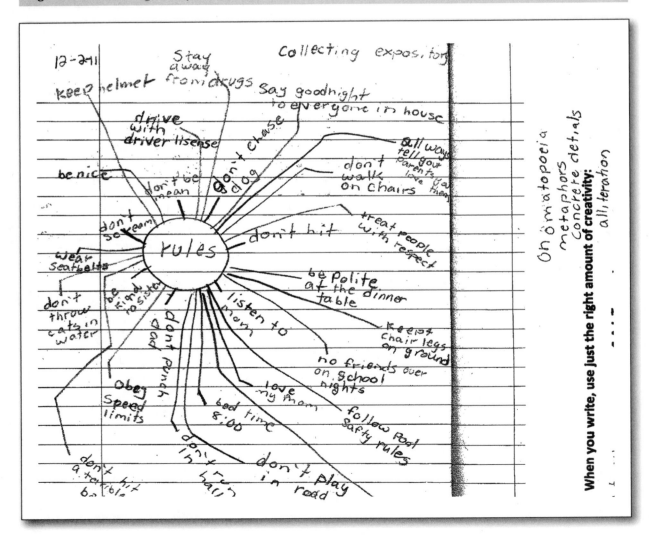

Stroll Down Memory Lane

Excellent for: Narrowing Topics

This prewriting activity helps students whittle broad topics into manageable writing ideas. For this strategy, let me give you a concrete example. At the beginning of the year, my students and I create an anchor chart of possible topics to write about. This list includes, pets, grandparents, holidays, fears, and so forth. These are very broad. When I introduce the Memory Lane strategy, I take one of those broad topics and narrow it down to small and specific moments or ideas.

Pets (from the anchor chart of topics)

- My first dog Scruffie
  **The day I bought Scruffie from a pet store
- My daily walks with Scruffie
  **The day we were chased by a pack of dogs during a walk
- The times Scruffie got in trouble
  **The day Scruffie ate my favorite pair of shoes

I use this example with my students so that they can see how each time I started off broad (my first dog Scruffie) I needed to think of something more specific (the day I bought Scruffie from a pet store). The stroll down Memory Lane strategy is the perfect way to teach students to narrow down their possibilities. With my sample above, I actually have three narrative possibilities to write about. The more ways I show my students how to collect ideas, the less times I hear "I have nothing to write about."

Heart Mapping

Excellent for: Discovering Ideas That Resonate

A simple heart, drawn in the middle of a page in a writer's notebook, can help students brainstorm places, people, food, and memories that they love (Figure 6.3). If it's important to a student, it can go inside that heart. By simply adding these entries, a student has created a place filled with potential ideas for all types of writing. I find that many of my students like to draw as well as list things that they love in the heart map. I have no problem with quick sketches and I clarify for my students that any sketches serve a purpose—to generate ideas. These quick sketches should always be accompanied by labels and are not overly detailed like an illustration would be. For younger writers, I would suggest providing them with a heart template to make it a little easier to create the map.

Hand Mapping

Excellent for: Kinesthetic Idea Generation and Planning

Barry Lane, in his book, *Writing a Road to Self-Discovery*, explains the hand map as a prewriting strategy that can help students bring memories to a conscious level. These memories are based on emotional triggers that each finger on the hand represents. I ask

Figure 6.3 Heart Mapping Example

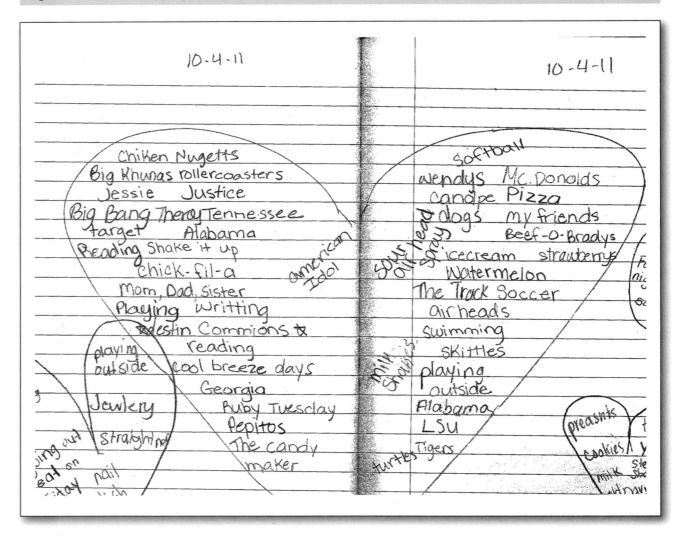

my students to trace their hand on a page in their writer's notebooks. I show them my example as well (Figure 6.4). Any emotion can be used, but to start off the year, I use the following: scared, nervous, happy, excited, and angry. One emotion is written on each finger. The next step is to have students recall memories from their lives that represent each emotion. These memories are written as spokes (much like on a web) extending from each finger.

Noticings

Excellent for: Elaborating on Ideas

Real writers notice the world around them. I want my students to take a moment and begin to view their world through the eyes of a writer. One strategy that I use is a sensory noticings chart. This chart can be used during a field trip to the zoo, sitting in a hammock in their own backyard, or while on a simple tour of the school and the grounds. It is amazing what students notice when they sit and really make themselves

Figure 6.4 Hand Mapping Example

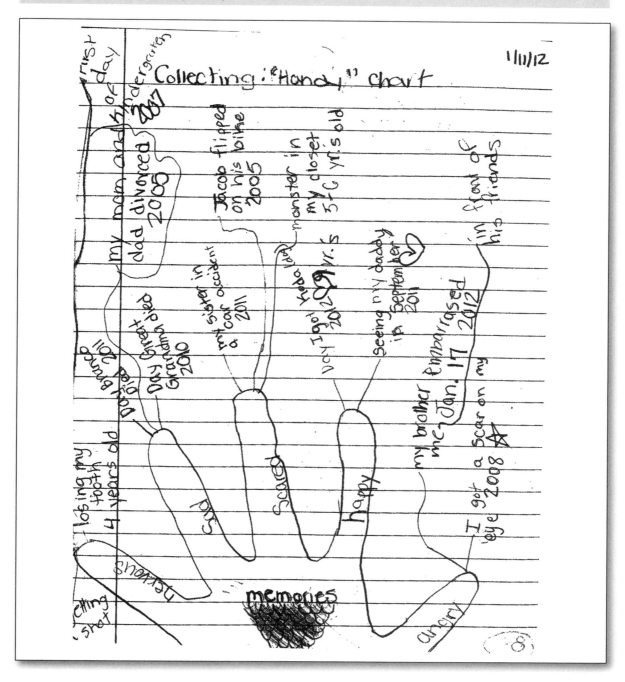

aware of their surroundings. I do ask, the first time we tour the school and grounds, that there is no talking. I want the focus to be on the sensory noticings and chit-chatting with a friend may hinder the results of this strategy. I also have these charts readily available to my students who may wish to take one home and record their noticings. We do not always focus on the sensory details that we notice. I want my students to understand that just reflecting on the world around you, in whatever fashion, is a strategy that real writers use. A student may choose to list what they notice or put it in a web. I leave these types of decisions up to my students.

Writing Back

Excellent for: Generating and Sequencing Ideas

This particular prewriting strategy is one of my favorite ways for collecting ideas and has proven to be a favorite of my students as well. I show my students my numerous writing back lists and timelines that have sparked some seed ideas and made their way to publication. My students are asked to go on a journey, with their mind, and remember things that happened in their lives (Figure 6.5). I don't require that these events are sequentially correct, that is not how our brains work. Just getting down my memories is important. I ask that if they can remember how old they were when this memory occurred, to please put it out beside the entry. Our goal is to see how far back we can go with our memories. I show my students, through my own example in my notebook, how the furthest I have been able to remember moments is at four years old. This strategy is difficult at first. But the more times my students revisit their list and add to it, the easier the memories seem to surface. After the students have several memories listed, and this could take several different occasions of remembering, I like for them to use the bulleted entries and put them in a timeline organizer that I provide for them. This is a great way for them to not only put specific events in order but to see which times in their lives they could remember more about and times they may not have been able to recall much. Patterns of memories also emerge. For example, some students remember moments that happened in their lives based on holidays and birthdays while other students are pretty well-rounded in all aspects of their day-to-day living. *One note*: Many times students who may leave out chunks of time from their lives may indicate that this was a difficult time for them and this is ok. But sometimes you have students who are ready to revisit these moments and may even choose to write about them. I am accepting of whatever it is my students may need, emotionally, and never push or prod, but they know I am there for them.

ABC Quilt

Excellent for: Generating Ideas and Organization

Writing is about choices as well as keeping these choices categorized. A simple ABC quilt pattern organizer helps my students; they enjoy the challenge of brainstorming topics based on each letter of the alphabet. This is an on-going process that lasts all year long. I like to model how to use the ABC quilt with an example of my own on chart paper. I periodically add to it when new topics come to mind and this reinforces the students to do the same. A variation of this strategy is to simply ask the students to create a chart in their writer's notebook listing the ABCs from the top line to the bottom line, one letter per line. Their ideas can still be categorized and the concept is the same, except nothing has to be photocopied. If I use the quilt pattern I still have my students glue the organizer into their notebooks. That way the information doesn't get lost. One tidbit of advice, make sure they use glue sticks, and just a dab, or it will be difficult to write on.

Walking the Path With My Students

I believe that if I had a motto for classroom teachers it would be, "Always walk the same path you ask your students to walk." It is my firm belief that to be an effective

Figure 6.5 Writing Back Example

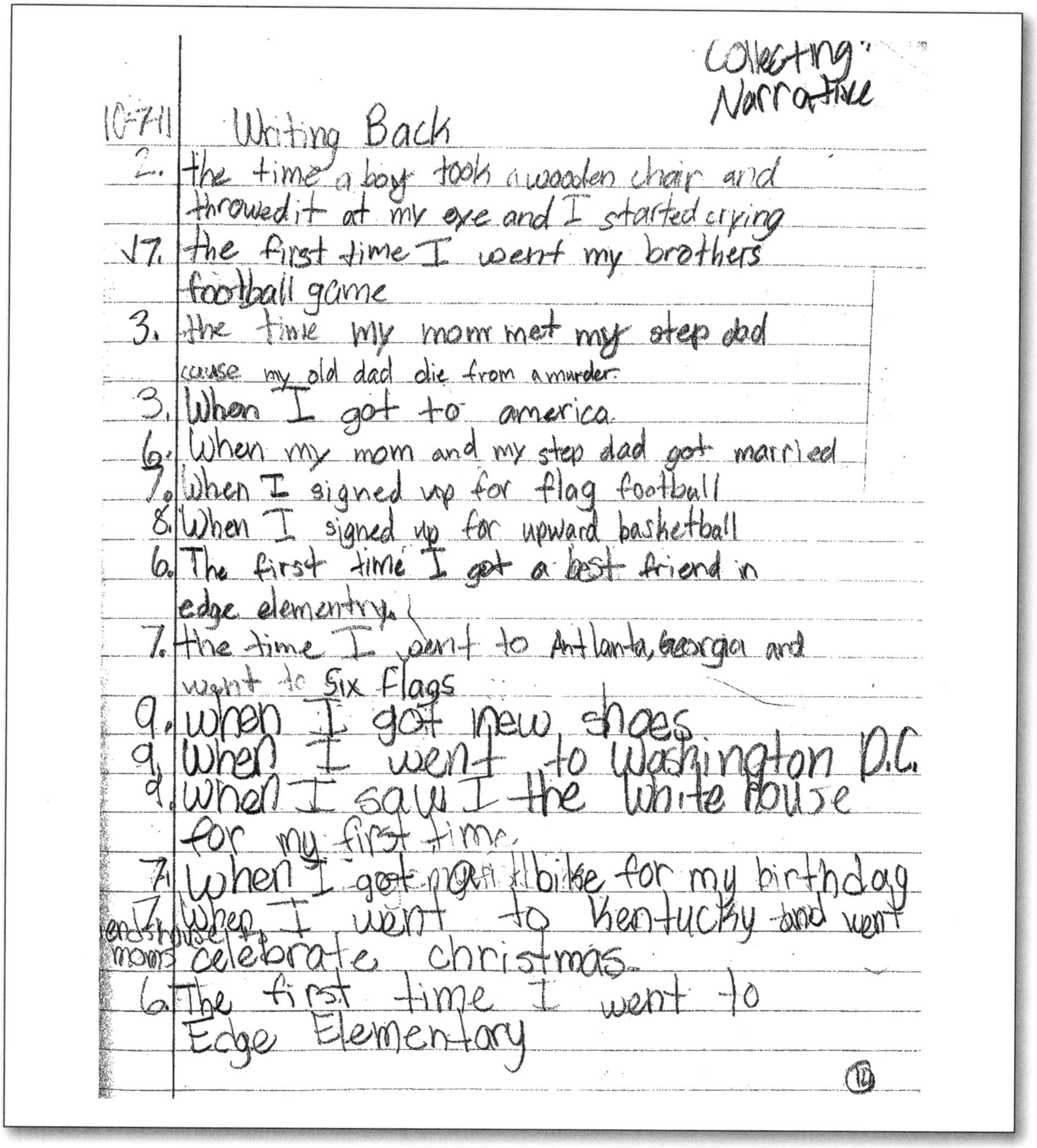
Collecting: Narrative

10-7-11 Writing Back

2. the time a boy took a wooden chair and throwed it at my eye and I started crying
√7. the first time I went my brothers football game
3. the time my mom met my step dad cause my old dad die from a murder.
3. When I got to america
6. When my mom and my step dad got married
7. When I signed up for flag football
8. When I signed up for upward basketball
6. The first time I got a best friend in edge elementry.
7. the time I went to Antlanta, Georgia and went to Six Flags
9. when I got new shoes
9. When I went to Washington D.C.
9. when I saw I the White House for my first time.
7. When I got a ... bike for my birthday
7. When I went to Kentucky ~~and went~~ moms ... house celebrate christmas.
6. The first time I went to Edge Elementary

14

writing teacher, I must try, at least once, what it is I am asking my students to do. If I ask for them to have a writer's notebook, I have one. If I ask for them to draw a heart map in their notebooks and add people, places, and things that they love, I must show them my own example first so they can see I have also tried out the strategy. This is important to me, as well as my students, because if we are going to be a community of writers then we all need to work hard, take risks, and trust each other . . . myself included. This, to me, is especially critical when it comes time to plan.

PLANNING

"In writing, there is first a creating stage—a time you look for ideas, you explore, you cast around for what you want to say. Like the first phase of building, this creating stage is full of possibilities."

—Ralph Waldo Emerson

Inverted Triangle

Excellent for: Narrowing Down a Topic or Idea

One problem I have found with my students' writing is that their topics are too broad. For example, instead of writing a story about a terrifying roller coaster ride, the student's writing sounds more like a list of everything he or she did at the theme park. One strategy I use to help students narrow down their focus is the inverted triangle. The inverted triangle helps my struggling writers visually see their stories and determine the main moments of the story, not just list. The layers of the triangle can vary according to the student. For example, I like to start with four sections in the triangle. My goal is to help my students recognize the "it" moment. Here is a sample in Figure 6.6. If you are like me, I am very visual and sometimes a picture is worth *more* than a thousand words.

Figure 6.6 Inverted Triangle Example

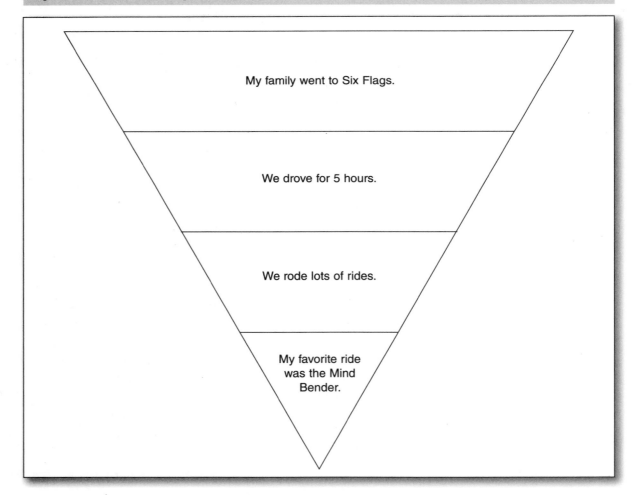

My family went to Six Flags.

We drove for 5 hours.

We rode lots of rides.

My favorite ride was the Mind Bender.

The real story here is the moment on the roller coaster. That time of excitement and fear. I want this student to really focus on this moment. I call this moment the "it" moment or the "hover" moment. Stay at that spot for awhile. Don't rush the details, the emotions, and the fun! Yes, the other parts of the triangle are important, maybe in the introduction of a personal narrative. But the majority of the paper should focus on the ride.

Storm and Sort

Excellent for: Planning Beginning, Middle, and End

Brainstorming is a critical part of writing. I have found, however, that my students are unaware of just what to do with the information they have brainstormed. If we are brainstorming for ideas, the concept is pretty clear. If we are brainstorming as part of the planning process, the concept becomes a little foggy. I simply ask my student to try and remember as many details, facts, important moments, and so on, that they can remember related to their story or essay (Figure 6.7). After the initial brainstorming with either a list or a web, I show my students how to categorize this information. Let me use a personal narrative example.

I typically start with a web when I first introduce brainstorming to my students. But a web is just a web. So I take the process a little deeper. I ask them to draw three columns on their planning page. We label one section a B for *beginning*, the middle section M for *middle*, and the last section and E for *ending*. I model how I have also brainstormed with a web and then took the details from my web and transferred them to where they fall in the story. If a detail belongs in the beginning of the story (possibly details about character, setting, problem, etc.) then the students transfer the information from the web to the beginning column in the chart. Typically any action or what I referred to earlier (in the inverted triangle strategy) will go in the middle column of the planning page. For the ending column, my students usually transfer details that had to do with a problem solved, a final thought, or memory. It doesn't take as long as it may appear to have students transfer information from the web to the three column chart. It gives students a visual. The middle column should have the most amount of details because it is the middle where everything really happens in a personal narrative. And since we draft right after we plan, I'd much rather my students see any potential problems before they draft (for example the middle is lacking in action).

Bold Beginning	Mighty Middle	Excellent End

Figure 6.7 Storm and Sort Example

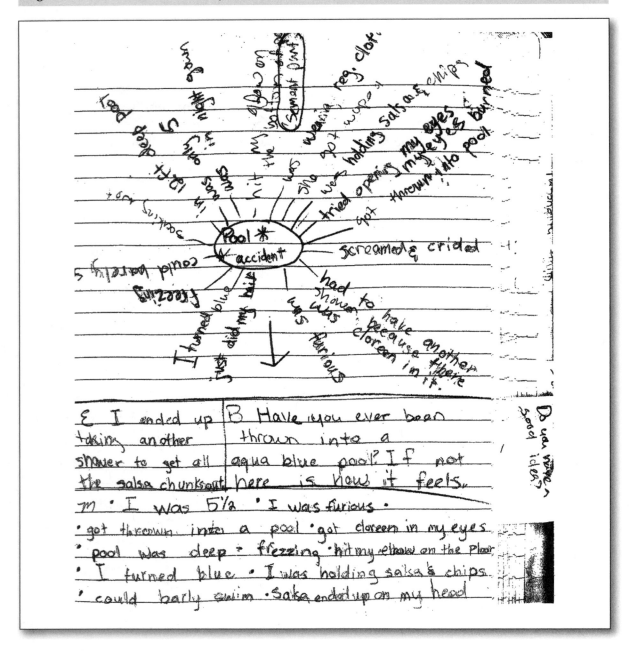

Quick Sketch

Excellent for: Kinesthetic and Visual Learners/ Recalling Details

Students love to draw. And for our struggling writers, anything visual seems to help them. The purpose of this strategy is for students to recall details of specific characters in their stories or to go back to the hover moment and recall the action and emotion that was evident (Figure 6.8). I like to share with my students how a quick sketch (or often called a quick draw) helped me with one of my recent stories I had published. I was working on a piece about a chocolate Lab named Tootsie. I wanted to start the personal narrative with a description of Tootsie. So I sat down and drew a quick sketch. After I drew the quick sketch I labeled all of the details that I knew would help my story. I labeled the triangular ears, the silvery muzzle, and the delightful girth that had earned Tootsie her name (she looked just like a Tootsie Roll). This strategy works great for a narrative or an expository piece of writing. For a narrative story, the characters and setting are often sketched and labeled. For an expository piece, a quick sketch with labeling is useful when students are researching animals or space craft, and so on, and specific parts are labeled like in a diagram.

Figure 6.8 Quick Sketch Example

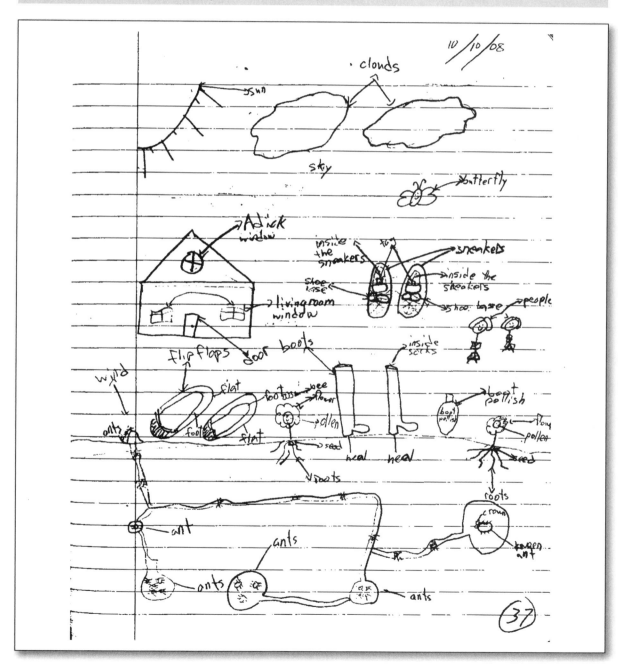

Storyboard

Excellent for: Sequencing Narratives

One of the things I love the most about the storyboard is how easy this strategy is to differentiate. A storyboard is simply squares drawn in a writer's notebook or a piece of notebook paper. For my more advanced students, a storyboard may consist of 6 to 7 boxes, but for my struggling writers, 3 to 4 boxes seem to work best. As my struggling writers become more confident in their abilities, I see them adding more boxes to their storyboards and their writing is filled with more action and details. Each square is dedicated to an event from their story. The storyboard helps students organize and sequence their stories. I have also let my students use large sticky notes instead of drawing squares, so that the storyboard becomes a moveable piece of writing. It lets the students manipulate the sequence and play around with the events until they are in the correct order.

I like to model this strategy a couple of times before my students plan their own stories. I use a simple picture book to help illustrate my point. As I read the book, we identify the major parts of the story. It is a great visual for students if you write each part with a different colored marker. Let me elaborate a little. If we are working on a personal narrative, I remind my students that a narrative has three main parts, a beginning (I use a green marker), middle (I use a blue marker), and an end (I use a red marker). As I read the mentor text we look closely at the main events. You can use chart paper for this activity, but I simply use my white board and three different colored pens. By the time the story is finished my students can identify the main parts of the story, in order, as well as categorized based on parts. Since the middle is where most of the action and events take place, the students will clearly see that most of the boxes have been written with a blue pen.

Chain of Events/Y Map

Excellent for: Revising a Piece of Writing for Details

Sensory details are important in all types of writing. One strategy that I teach my students is the Y chart. I ask my students to draw a large capital Y in their writer's notebook. You could also ask them to do this on a planning page you may provide. Each section is labeled with one of the five senses. This Y map can change depending on the senses needed for a piece of writing. For example, if I have a student writing a story about a picnic with the family, the Y map may focus on the senses of sight, smell, and hearing. If another student is writing a story about his birthday party, the Y map may focus on the senses of taste, sight, and touch. The Y map can also be used for an expository piece of writing. In this case, the senses may not necessarily be used to categorize the sections. If a student is writing an essay on the great white shark, the Y map may focus on what it eats, where it lives, and how it hunts its prey.

After the sections of the Y map are labeled, the students think of details or facts that have to do with each section. The student who wrote about the picnic will list everything he saw, smelled, and heard and the Y map keeps these details categorized. The student who used the Y map for the great white shark piece would list facts pertaining to the three areas (eating, habitat, and hunting) and use them to write the central paragraphs that are required for this type of writing.

E Chart

Excellent for: Organizing Details in Expository Writing

I cannot begin to count the number of times I have asked my students to elaborate further on the three central paragraphs of their expository essays. So I came up with a quick and effective solution to this problem. Since elaboration begins with an "E" I tried to think of what I needed to see my students including in those central three paragraphs of an essay. I model for my students this process on a piece of chart paper. To start this strategy, I draw a large "E" on the piece of chart paper. I title the chart Elaboration. The top line of the E is for explanations, the middle line of the E is for examples, and the last line of the E is for experiences. This becomes an excellent planning page. The process is repeated three times, once for each of the three central paragraphs in an expository essay. Each of these three paragraphs needs to be elaborated with explanations (why this is important), examples (facts to support the topic sentence), and personal experiences (one time I. . .). My students love this strategy, and I have found that there is more life and creativity in the essays as well as personality.

Story Star: Naming the Story Problem

The best personal narratives and fiction stories involve some kind of challenge a main character overcomes. Without that, the story lacks tension. You can help young writers understand that by doing a minilesson that shows them a *somebody/wanted/but/ so/how* sequence. Point it out in picture books, too. The character wants or desires something, someone or some internal obstacle stands in the way, the character experiences events and overcomes the obstacle, and grows in some way so that he no longer needs what he was yearning for.

Students also respond to a *somebody/wanted/but/so/how* sequence if each is framed as a question a reporter or detective is posing, and we visualize them as points on a sheriff's star. And if your students aren't quite ready to adequately handle story obstacles, you can simplify it with *who, what, when, where, and how.*

Here's how it would go. I show them how to draw a large star in the middle of the piece of paper—and ask them to use their writer's notebook, where all their planning occurs. There are five points to a star. Inside each point we write one of the five reporter questions. Outside of the point is where we answer *who* the story is about, *where* does the story take place, *how* does the story end, *what* happens in the story (main events), and finally, *when* does the story take place (past, present, season, year, etc.). This plan is very helpful when it comes time to draft. When I taught younger grades, I would help the students create their own story stars out of yellow construction paper and Popsicle sticks. These stars were kept at their desks for easy access when it came time to write. My students planned verbally and they used the stars to guide their storytelling. My older students actually write out the answers to the questions on their planning page.

DRAFTING

"The beautiful thing about writing is that you don't have to get it right the first time, unlike, say, a brain surgeon."

Robert Cormier

For the stage of drafting, I do not have strategies, per se, rather general advice that is still presented as minilessons. I also have a folder full of my own efforts with drafting that I readily share with my students. Many of these drafts have found their way to publication and this inspires my students. Much of the advice about drafting that I provide my students comes from favorite authors like Jan Brett, Jane Yolen, and others. I like to use quotes to help the students see how critical this step of the process is. I find it helpful to give my students a simple reference chart with tips for drafting. Because my class uses the writer's notebook, this chart is glued in the back of the notebook, to be used as a reference whenever it is needed. It is important for students to make connections with themselves and the writing process. For struggling students, the connections they make build self-esteem. There is comfort among students when they realize that real writers make mistakes and that perfection is not part of the process, trial and error is. Here is a sample of the chart I give my students.

Tips for Drafting

1. Read examples of the genre you are writing.

2. Don't expect a perfect piece of writing. A rough draft is supposed to be rough.

3. Set small goals and know that you will have time to work on your draft.

4. Write in a natural style . . . your own voice.

5. Sometimes it is easier to start in the middle than at the beginning.

6. Take a break after you have drafted, preferably overnight, before you start to revise.

7. Read your draft aloud. Use the whisper phones* if that helps.

8. Ask a writing partner to read your draft and fill out a *What I Liked/Why* T-chart.

9. Remember to skip lines and do not write on the back of pages. You will need the space later when you revise.

---

*A whisper phone is an acoustical voice-feedback headset that can help students read quietly out loud without disturbing others. They can be purchased at most educational sites or catalogues.

Drafting is one step closer to publication, and it serves an important role to the writer, getting thoughts on paper. I explain to my students that writers have several drafts. The first time a writer drafts, his or her main goal is to get the information down. After all, the idea has already been selected and planned, so now it's time to take the next step. In my classroom, we do not use our plans or notes or research the first time we draft. Many times students are handicapped in their efforts because their main concern turns from writing down their draft with a free flow of thoughts to stopping and checking their plans for every detail. This slows down the drafting process. Donald Murray (1968), in his book *A Writer Teaches Writing*, elaborates this point when he says "The writer should put aside all notes while writing a first draft. What is remembered is usually what should be remembered, and what is forgotten is usually what should be left out" (54). The notes and planning are re-introduced the next day after the initial draft is complete. My students are usually amazed by how much of their story they remembered but enjoy having the opportunity to review their plan. This review gives their plan purpose when important parts or details are applied to the existing draft. Plus, I point out to my students that a good plan leads to a good draft. It helps you sort and organize what you'd like to say before you write it down.

Freeze and Question

One strategy that I like to use, every now and then, to break up any monotony in the drafting process is called "freeze and question." Midway through a first draft, I will have students freeze and stop their writing, no matter where they may be in their draft. I do let them know ahead of time that we will be using this strategy for the day. It motivates some students, who may often drag the drafting stage out, to work a little faster so that they will have something to share with a partner. After I say "Freeze," the students walk around and find a partner to read their draft to. Partner 1 reads his or her draft to Partner 2 and then Partner 2 has the opportunity to ask any questions he or she may have about the piece of writing. The process is then repeated with Partner 2 reading his or her draft and Partner 1 asking questions. All of the students are asked to return to their seats and continue drafting. By getting up and moving around and sharing, a new energy is often sensed and the questions the writers were asked by their partners gives them direction and focus on areas that may need a little work. Being able to discuss each other's writing, using specific and appropriate language, is a foundational tool that, not just struggling writers, but all writers, need in order to recognize and apply the craft techniques that make good writing good.

Sharing

Sharing after a draft is critical because it gives students the chance to learn from each other as well as a safety stop for any questions that might be had, by the reader or the writer, before the next steps toward publication occur. It allows students time to rehearse their story before revision, editing, and publishing come in to play. One strategy I use for sharing that helps give my students a boost of confidence before taking another step toward publication is a simple *What I Liked and Why* T-chart. I keep these charts in a basket at the front of the room. When two students complete a draft, they partner up and retrieve one of the T-charts. The goal for this strategy is for one writer to receive positive feedback from another and vice versa. This positive feedback does wonders for the self-esteem of all writers. Struggling writers, in particular, may have feeling of inadequacy when it comes to their abilities as a writer. The simple act of having another student's praise, even the simplest of efforts, brings the level of accomplishment up a little. I truly believe it is one of the reasons my students like to write . . . they feel like they can do it and are actually good at it. I have always heard that the first battle to teaching writing is to get the students to like it. I have no problems in that area, and I give these methods for sharing credit for helping my students feel successful. Here is an example of a completed *What I Liked and Why* T-chart.

Writer: Bill

Partner: Susie

What I Liked	Why
• The word stumbled	• It is a stronger verb than fell
• "YEOWWW!"	• Grabbed my attention
• Slowly slipped sideways	• Alliteration adds fluency and rhythm
• I saw. I liked. I bought.	• 3 short sentences sped up the moment in the story

Open–Ended Questions

Sometimes it is necessary to provide students with a list of open-ended questions that can help the writing partner know how to compliment the writer. This is not necessarily a natural occurrence. It takes time to become familiar with the language that writers use. Here are a few of those open-ended questions that can spark comments on the T-chart:

- What did you like about the writing?
- Were there any similes or metaphors?
- Did the beginning grab your attention? How?
- What words or phrases stood out?
- Did the writing have an emotional impact on you? How?
- Was the ending satisfying? How?
- Was there evidence of strong verbs in the writing?
- Were you able to locate _____? (Any of the above listed craft techniques could be used to fill in this blank).

The purpose of sharing is two-fold. It helps the writer celebrate the successful moments of writing in his or her paper and it helps the writing partner learn to notice and name qualities of good writing. The open-ended questions can serve as a guide until the language is better understood and more techniques are taught and recognized. It is, to me, a win-win situation.

REVISING

"Good writing is essentially revision. I am positive of this."

—Roald Dahl

The definition of revision is "to see again" and I like to add "preferably with fresh eyes." After my students complete their draft, find a writing partner to share and celebrate with, we leave our piece of writing for a day. As a writer myself, I know that I have more energy to revisit a draft when I have put it aside for a day. When we do come back to our drafts, we grab our blue pens and focus on improving our draft.

Revision is seen as a direct loop to direct instruction in craft. Just as a woodworker uses many tools and techniques to craft a piece of furniture, a skilled writer uses tools and techniques of language to craft a piece of writing. Writing craft is a broad term for how a writer intentionally uses techniques to create meaning and feeling for the reader. The following list is a small sample of the techniques I teach my students through revising minilessons.

Revising Mini-Lessons

- Similes
- Brilliant beginnings
- Exceptional endings
- Onomatopoeia
- Alliteration
- Anadiplosis
- Strong verbs
- Adding emotions
- Slowing down the "it" moment (climax)
- Removing unnecessary information
- Adding or deleting a part

This list of craft is generated through the help of my students. Before we revise, we brainstorm what good writers do when they revise. Children tend to confuse revising with editing, so having an anchor chart for them to refer to decreases that confusion. I also ask that this list of craft lessons is recorded in my students' writer's notebooks so they have their own reference available at any time.

What Good Writers Do When They Revise

- Change sentences
- Add words

- Pump up boring words
- Reread, reread, reread
- Answer all of the reader's questions
- Remove sentences
- Add sentences
- Rearrange sentences
- Check and recheck

The following poster helps student remember the basics of revising.

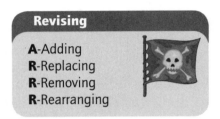

Another strategy I use to keep revising and editing separate is the use of different colored pens. When students are revising, they use a blue pen. The anchor chart above is written in blue pen as well. When my students edit, they use a red pen.

I like to provide my students with the following chart that helps them see the differences and purposes of revising and editing.

REVISING is like remodeling a house because you may . . .

1. Knock out a wall (or a paragraph)

2. Join two rooms together (or combine sentences)

3. Put in a new window (or clarify ideas)

4. Sculpt the walls with Spanish lace (or add creativity strategies)

5. EDITING is the cleaning or straightening up (or fine tuning for the reader and the presentation)

Revision Checklists

Teachers typically provide students with editing checklists. But what about when students are revising? I like to show my students how to create their own personalized revising checklists using sticky notes. I generally teach 3 to 4 craft lessons each time my students reach the stage of revising. It is important that students have a working draft in order to try out and apply not only the revising lesson but editing ones as well. The first time my students revise a draft, I look at the list of craft techniques and decide which ones to teach for the next few days. It is a basic research, decide, and teach method. I *research* the present draft and other pieces of writing that my students have worked on, then *decide* which areas of writing need improving, and then I create lessons to *teach* that will focus on those specific areas.

Once I have taught several revising lessons and students have had the opportunity to fix up their drafts, I ask for them to look at the anchor chart on the wall and select one or two additional examples of craft that they need to apply to their draft. I pass out sticky notes, and the students create revising checklists based on what they feel their draft still needs. Because I do want to see evidence that the lessons I have taught them are also being applied, I ask that those examples of craft are listed first and accounted for. Let me give you a specific example of this method.

A Conversational Journey

Me: Students, over the last few days we have worked hard revising our drafts. I would like one of my writers to remind us of a craft technique we learned about through our minilessons?

Bill: Ms. Morris, you showed us how to add strong verbs to our drafts.

Me: Thank you, Bill, that is correct. Strong verbs are those active verbs that paint a picture for our readers. I need another writer to help us review. Remember how we studied the book, *The Bee Tree*, by Patricia Polacco? We found so many strong verbs for *ran* and *chased*.

Susan: We learned that writers add emotion words to their stories to help the reader feel what they are feeling. I still remember when we read and studied the book, *How are You Peeling? Foods with Moods*, by Saxton Freymann. That was a funny book.

Me: Good point, Susan. Emotions and feelings are very important for the reader to experience. We learned one more technique writers use when they revise, what is it?

Linda: Writers use onomatopoeia, or sound words, and that is my favorite technique we got to try.

Me: That is an excellent job, Linda. I admit I am a fan of onomatopoeia myself. Our next step is to add these three craft techniques to our revising checklists. Let's do that right now.

_____Strong Verbs
_____Emotion words
_____Onomatopoeia

At this point, my students add to their checklists and it now looks something like this:

Me: I like how all of my writers have this information on their checklist. Now I would like for you to look at the chart we created earlier in the year, *"What Good Writers Do When They Revise."* Please select one or two more techniques that you feel your paper needs and add those to your checklist.

_____Strong Verbs
_____Emotion Words
_____Onomatopoeia
_____Sensory Details
_____Alliteration

Let me use Linda's checklist as an example:

Me: I am so proud of how hard my writers are working. I would like for you to go on a scavenger hunt. The place you are searching through is your draft. The tools you may use are the blue pen and your checklist. And what you are hunting for are examples of craft that you already see in your draft or areas where you can add the craft techniques you have on your checklist. Please remember to give yourself a check on the line if you discover examples of craft and when you add moments of craft.

XXXXX Strong Verbs

XX_____ Emotion Words

XXXX_ Onomatopoeia

XXXX_ Sensory Details

X_____ Alliteration

After several minutes, Linda's checklist looks like this. As you can see she has found or added:

- Five examples of strong verbs
- Two examples of emotion words
- Four examples of onomatopoeia
- Four examples of sensory details
- One example of alliteration

Revising Cubes

I love the versatility of the revising cubes (Figure 6.9). For these cubes, I simply write six ways that students can revise their work. I make sure that I have modeled and have explicitly taught these ways before allowing the students to use this tool independently. There are so many skills used when a student (or writer) revises. I listed a few of the minilessons I teach about revising earlier in this chapter. Any of the revising minilessons can be written on the cube. My cubes change as my instruction changes. Here are some additional minilessons for the stage of revising that can be taught and then added to the revising cube.

Additional Revising Strategies

- Synonyms for *said* (*Stellaluna by* Janelle Cannon and *The Bee Tree* by Patricia Polacco are excellent books to use)
- Linking verbs
- Creating internal rhymes (*I Ain't Gonna Paint No More* by Karen Beaumont is an excellent book for teaching this skill)
- Sensory details
- Adding dialogue
- Writerly 3 (*It was a sad, sad, sad day.*)
- Show don't tell
- Metaphors
- Personification

RULES OF REVISION

- Build on strength
- Cut what can be cut
- Simplicity is best
- The writing will tell you how to write

Figure 6.9   Revising Cubes

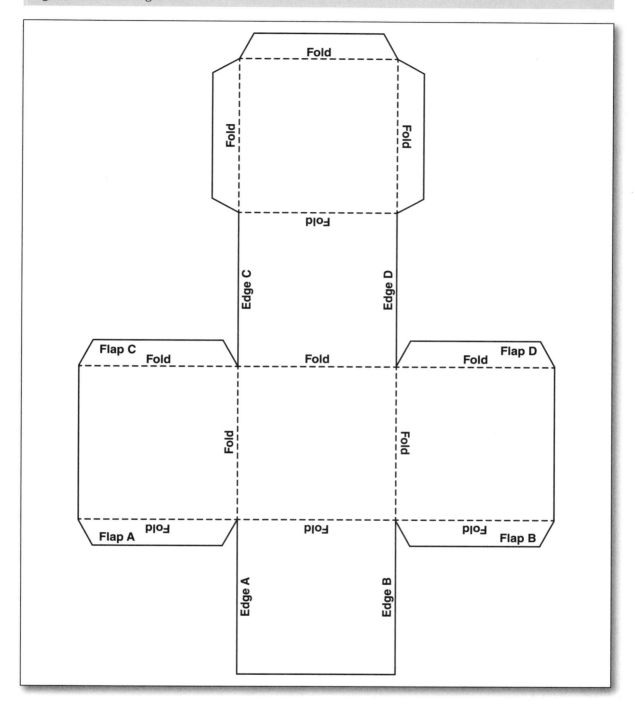

Three Different Types of Reading for Revision:

FIRST READ: **FOCUS** (my pen is capped ☺)

- What does the piece of writing mean?
- Are all the reader's questions answered?

- Is new information needed?
- Is the genre appropriate to the meaning?
- Are there any examples that can be cut loose?
- Is there a section that should be a separate piece of writing?
- Is each point supported by convincing evidence?
- Is the piece long enough to satisfy the reader?
- Is the piece short enough to keep the reader involved?

SECOND READING: **FORM** (my pen comes off . . . but slowly ☺)

- Is the title on target?
- Does the lead catch the reader . . . in 3 seconds or less?
- Does the lead deliver on its contract with the reader?
- Does the piece answer the reader's questions at the point the reader will ask them?
- How can I get out of the way of the reader and show rather than tell?
- Is there variety in my creativity?
- Does the piece reinforce the meaning?
- Does the pace provide enough energy to carry the reader forward?
- Are the sections proportionate to each other?

THIRD READING: **VOICE** (my pen is fully uncapped ☺)

- Can the piece be read aloud?
- Are important pieces of specific information at the ends and beginnings of paragraphs?
- Does each paragraph make one point?
- Does each paragraph carry a full load of meaning to the reader?
- Do the paragraphs vary in length in relation to meaning?
- Are the paragraphs in order?
- Does the reader leave each sentence with more information than when the reader entered it?
- Are there sentences that can be cut?
- Are most sentences subject-verb-object sentences? (short sentences communicate)
- Are there clauses that get in the way of meaning?
- Are the verbs active and strong enough?
- Has the right word been found?
- Does the meaning depend on verbs and nouns, not adverbs and adjectives?
- Can the writing be more specific?
- Are there unnecessary forms of the verb "to be?"
- Is every fact checked?
- Is each word spelled correctly?
- Is there anything I can do to make the writing simple? Clear? Graceful? Accurate? Fair?

Do you ask yourself all of these questions in every piece of writing? NO!! These areas are internalized and they overlap. A writer must work back and forth from meaning to focus to form to voice and from voice to form to focus to meaning.

Source: Information is based on the article *Making Meaning Clear* by Donald M. Murray.

EDITING

"Proofread carefully to see if you any words out."

—Author Unknown

Editing is a courtesy to the reader. It is that final spit and polish writers do before publication. I give my students the following chart to help them be better prepared to fix up their own writing at any stage of the process. This chart is simple advice and a quick reference for students to use whenever they deem necessary.

Quick Tips for Fixing Up Your Writing

- If it works, leave it alone.
- K.I.S.S.: Keep it simple students.
- Aim for simplicity.
- If it can be cut, cut it.
- Make the verbs as active as possible.
- Make the nouns as concrete as possible.
- Elaborate on main characters with traits and actions.
- Use quotations to give authority.
- Make the piece factual or personal.
- Correct conventions are a courtesy to the reader. (spelling, grammar, punctuation)

CUPS

Just like with the stage of revising, I show my students an effective way to create an editing checklist with the acronym CUPS. Remember that when my students edit, they use the red pens to help differentiate between revising and editing. The anchor chart that I create uses the same color-coded method.

As students look over and re-read their drafts for each section on the editing checklist, they give themselves a check or an "x" as a way to celebrate that they have not only checked but corrected what was needed. I put this version of our editing checklist on a large piece of chart paper. I like to have visual aids displayed and readily available for any students who need them. I typically do not make copies of this checklist, I provide sticky notes and the students create their own editing checklist using the example that is on the chart paper. Here is an example of what a student sample would look like after editing is complete.

CUPS

Capitalization _____
Usage _____
Punctuation _____
Spelling _____

C ___ (add ✓ ✓ ✓ ✓ checks)
U ___ (add ✓ check)
P ___ (add ✓ ✓ ✓ ✓ ✓ ✓ checks)
S ___ (add ✓ ✓ ✓ ✓ ✓ checks)

Copy-Cover-Compare

The only materials you need for this strategy are paper and pencils. My students use writer's notebooks so these strategies are practiced in the notebooks. I ask my students to create three columns by drawing two vertical lines evenly apart. The columns are labeled *copy, cover, compare*. Because I want my students to misspell fewer and fewer words each time they edit, I need to make sure that as they identify and correct misspelled words in their drafts, that we take the time to learn the correct spelling. This does not require a formal spelling test each week. What I love about this strategy is everyone has a differentiated set of words that they need to work on. As the students recognize and circle (with a red pen) the words in their drafts that they know are misspelled, I ask for them to look up the correct spelling of at least one-half of the words that are incorrect. Many times my students know how to spell the word; they just need to sound it out. But there are some words that need a little more practice. These are the words that I ask my students to look up. The students copy the correct spelling of the word in the first column labeled *copy*. After all of the words have been looked up in a dictionary, sight word list, or so on it is time to practice. I have the students look at one word at a time, whisper the correct spelling out loud, and trace the letters with their finger.

Next, the students cover the first column (we use 2-inch wide strips of construction paper) and in the middle column they write the word from memory. This attempt at spelling the word goes in the *cover* column. Finally, the students uncover the first column and compare the two spellings. The students correct any misspelled words in the third column (labeled *compare*). If a student spells a word correctly, I ask them to put a smiley face in the third column to celebrate. If a student misses the word, I ask them to add it to the bottom of the copy column to try again. This is a wonderful Tier 2 and Tier 3 activity for students who scored low on the correct letter sequences (CLS) probe. It is also good for our higher-level writers who want to practice adding more difficult words to their writing. Here is a sample of Jill's chart.

COPY	COVER	COMPARE
through	throgh	through
because	because	☺
against	aginst	against
through	through	☺
against	aginst	against

Jill is still struggling with the word against, so I know that this is a habitual misspelling and I need to give her more practice. I like for my students to make simple flashcards of these words that seem to give them a difficult time. They keep the cards in Ziploc bags and practice at any time during the day when an opportunity arises.

Editing Wheels

Another tool that I provide for my students, to assist with the editing process, is the editing wheel. These wheels can be differentiated based on the needs of your students. My expectations for the editing stage of the writing process may be different than those in a second grade classroom. I like for my students to have input into what good writers do during the editing process. We create an anchor chart and brainstorm what good writers do, then I use the brainstorming to create the editing wheels. My editing wheels change as my students learn more and more about the process of editing. The editing wheels I make and that the students use at the beginning of the year are different that the ones used toward the end of the year. My curriculum advances and constantly changes, so the tools my students use need to advance and change as well.

CLOSING THOUGHTS

I could not teach effectively without a buffet of strategies to choose from. Students learn in different ways and it is up to me, the classroom teacher, to expose them to many different ways to be successful. It is also important for my students to feel like independent writers. My goal for teaching with a variety of strategies and techniques is for students to have the tools necessary to solve problems that writers have. And these problems can occur within any stage of the process. I also want my students to have ownership over their writing and have significant on-task performance. By providing my students with reliable strategies, authentic techniques that writers use, and checklists and quotes to guide them along the way, I have helped lay the foundation for success, with even the students who seem to struggle the most.

References and Suggested Readings

Allington, R. (2009). *What really matters in response to intervention.* Boston, MA: Pearson.

Anderson, C. (2000). *How's it going? A practical guide to conferring with student writers.* Portsmouth, NH: Heinemann.

Applebaum, M. (2009). *The one-stop guide to implementing RTI.* Thousand Oaks, CA: Corwin.

Bender, W., & Shores, C. (2007). *Response to intervention: A practical guide for every teacher.* Thousand Oaks, CA: Corwin.

Benjamin, A. (2002). *Differentiated instruction: A guide for middle and high school teachers.* Larchmont, NY: Eye on Education.

Benjamin, A. (2003). *Differentiated instruction: A guide for elementary school teachers.* Larchmont, NY: Eye on Education.

Black, P., & William, D. (1998). Inside the black box: Raising standards through classroom assessment. *Phi Delta Kappan, 80*(2), 139–144.

Chapman C.. (2003). *Differentiated instructional strategies for writing in the content areas.* Thousand Oaks, CA: Corwin.

Culham, R. (2005). *6+1 Traits of Writing.* Portland, OR: Scholastic.

Drapeau, P. (2004). *Differentiated instruction: Making it work.* New York, NY: Scholastic.

Elbow, P. (1998). *Writing with power.* New York, NY: Oxford University.

Espin, C. A., De La Paz, S., Scierka, B. J., & Roelofs, L. (2005). The relationships between curriculum-based measures in written expression and quality and completeness of expository writing for middle school students. *The Journal of Special Education, 38,* 208–217.

Fisher, D. (2010). *Enhancing RTI: How to ensure success with effective classroom instruction and intervention.* Alexandria, VA: ASCD.

Fuchs, L. S., & Deno, S. L. (1994). Must instructionally useful performance assessment be based in the curriculum? *Exceptional Children, 61*(1), 15-24.

Fuchs, L. S., Fuchs, D., & Hamlett, C. L. (1989). Effects of instrumental use of Curriculum-Based Measurement to enhance instructional programs. *Remedial and Special Education, 10*(2), 43–52.

Fuchs, L. S., Fuchs, D., & Maxwell, L. (1988). The validity of informal reading comprehension measures. *Remedial and Special Education, 9,* 20–28.

Gregory, G. H. (2005*). Differentiating instruction with style: Aligning teacher and learner intelligence for maximum achievement.* Thousand Oaks, CA: Corwin.

Gregory, G. H., & Chapman, C. (2002). *Differentiated literacy strategies for student growth and achievement in Grades K-6.* Thousand Oaks, CA: Corwin.

Gudwin, D. (2010). *RTI.* Retrieved from http://denisegudwin.com/resources/rti/

Goldberg, G. (2002). *Reading, writing, and gender: Instructional strategies and classroom activities that work for girls and boys*. Larchmont, NY: Eye on Education.

Graves, D. (1983). *Writing: Teachers & children at work*. Portsmouth, NH: Heinemann.

Hollas, B. (2005). *Differentiated instruction in a whole-group setting*. Peterborough, NH: Crystal Springs.

Howard, M. (2009). *RTI from all sides*. Portsmouth, NH: Heinemann.

Lane, M. (1993). *Writing as a road to self-discovery*. Fairfield, OH: Writer's Digest.

Morris, L. (2012). *Awakening brilliance in the writer's workshop*. Larchmont, NY: Eye on Education.

Murray, D. (1968). *A writer teaches writing: A practical method of teaching composition*. Boston, MA: Houghton, Mifflin.

Murray, D. (1981). Making meaning clear. *Journal of Basic Writing, 88*.

Murray, D. (1982). *Learning by teaching: Selected articles on learning and teaching*. Montclair, NJ: Boynton/Cook.

Overmeyer, M. (2009). *What student writing teaches us*. Portland, MA: Stenhouse.

Paterson, K. (2005). *Differentiated learning: Language and literacy projects that address diverse backgrounds and cultures*. Markham, Ontario: Pembroke.

Shinn, M. R. (Ed.). (1998). *Advanced applications of curriculum-based measurement*. New York, NY: Guilford.

Shinn, M. R. (Ed.). (1998). *Advanced applications of curriculum-based measurement*. New York, NY: Guilford.

Slaughter, H. (2009). *Small-group writing conferences: How to use your instructional time*. Portsmouth, NH: Heinemann.

Strickland, D. (2002). *Supporting struggling readers and writers*. Portland, MA: Stenhouse.

Swearingen, R. (2002). *A primer: Diagnostic, formative, & summative assessment*. Toppenish, WA: Heritage University.

Tomlinson, C. *The differentiated classroom: Responding to the needs of all learners*. Alexandria, VA: ASCD.

Tomlinson, C. (2001). *How to differentiate instruction in mixed-ability classrooms*. Upper Saddle River, NJ: Pearson Education.

Tomlinson, C. *Differentiation in practice*. Alexandria, VA: ASCD.

Tomlinson, C., & Cunningham Eidson, C. (2003). *Differentiation in practice: A resource guide for differentiating curriculum: Grades K-5*. Alexandria, VA: ASCD.

Yatvin, J. (2004). *A room with a differentiated view: How to serve ALL children as individual learners*. Portsmouth, NH: Heinemann.

Index

CORWIN

A SAGE Company

The Corwin logo—a raven striding across an open book—represents the union of courage and learning. Corwin is committed to improving education for all learners by publishing books and other professional development resources for those serving the field of PreK–12 education. By providing practical, hands-on materials, Corwin continues to carry out the promise of its motto: **"Helping Educators Do Their Work Better."**